God Can Transform You
to Be Like Jesus

Jesus
by
heart

Roy Edgemon & Barry Sneed

LifeWay Press
Nashville, Tennessee

ISBN 0-7673-9851-3
Dewey Decimal Classification: 248.84
Subject Heading: Spiritual Life–Growth

This book is the text for course CG-0497
in the subject area Personal Life of the Christian Growth Study Plan.

Unless otherwise noted, Scripture quotations are from the Holy Bible, *New International Version*,
Copyright © 1973, 1978, 1984 by International Bible Society. Used by permission.
Other versions used:
King James Version (KJV).
New King James Version (NKJV). Copyright © 1979, 1980, 1982,
Thomas Nelson, Inc., Publishers. Used by permission.
THE MESSAGE. Copyright © by Eugene H. Peterson, 1993, 1994, 1995.
Used by permission of NavPress Publishing Group.

Cover Design: Edward Crawford and Tom Wright
Cover Illustration: Mike Wimmer

Printed in the United States of America

LifeWay Press
127 Ninth Avenue North
Nashville, Tennessee 37234-0150

Acknowledgments

The stories in this book are about real people — in particular about the life and character of Jesus Christ and how He transforms lives. From its conception, *Jesus by Heart* has been a special gift from God. He has used hundreds of godly minds to communicate shared wisdom throughout its pages. He has also guided a multitude of others to pray over each truth, labor over each sentence, and contribute in unique ways to each unit. Our heartfelt gratitude goes out to these individuals.

We also wish to acknowledge the dedicated efforts of Roy Edgemon, Henry Webb, Bill Taylor, Louis Hanks, Mike Miller, David Francis, John Kramp, and Ralph Hodge for their tireless commitment to the creation of the spiritual transformation document, which is the heartbeat of this book.

Words of special thanks go out to Ralph Hodge, who helped paint the vision for *Jesus by Heart*; to Ivey Harrington, who helped bring that vision to life; and to Sam House, who went the extra mile to create the leader's guide. We also wish to acknowledge with deepest gratitude the efforts of Henry Webb, who— like a faithful shepherd— guided us all every step of the way with a gentle hand and a voice filled with encouragement. The contributions of these special people were born out of their desire to see God transform people into the likeness of Jesus.

As we daily see lives transformed by God, we pause often to give thanks to our Heavenly Father, whose love for us was given life in the person of Jesus Christ. It is through Jesus that we come to know the heart of God, and it is through becoming like Jesus that our lives have true meaning and purpose.

Table of Contents

And we, who with unveiled faces

all reflect the Lord's glory,

are being transformed into his likeness

with ever-increasing glory,

which comes from the Lord,

who is the Spirit.

2 Corinthians 3:18

Therefore, I urge you, brothers,

in view of God's mercy,

to offer your bodies as living sacrifices,

holy and pleasing to God —

this is your spiritual act of worship.

Do not conform any longer

to the pattern of this world,

but be transformed

by the renewing of your mind.

Then you will be able to test and

approve what God's will is —

his good, pleasing and perfect will.

Romans 12:1-2

Dedication

To my wife Anna Marie, my best friend and partner in the ministry for almost 50 years. It has been a great joy to walk together, seeking to know Jesus by heart.

—Roy Edgemon

I dedicate this book to my wife Cindy. Because of her Christlike character and her incredible love for me, I am better able to understand spiritual transformation. She is my best friend and greatest asset in ministry and life.

—Barry Sneed

Start Here

A young soldier, who grew up in a fisherman's family on the banks of Lake Pontchartrain, said of his father's hard life. "My father was a Christian man. No matter how hard making a living fishing was, he never failed to give God credit for anything good, and he had ultimate faith that God was going to see us through when things were bad. I didn't pay much attention to his attempts to lead me to faith in Jesus when I was growing up. But after Papa died, I attended church and listened to the preacher describe Jesus and tell about His life. I was amazed and moved. I realized I'd already known a man like that — my Papa."[1]

To know "Papa" was to know Jesus. Unlike many Christians today, the old fisherman had known exactly what God wanted him to do with his life. He followed as his guide the truth Jesus proclaimed in John 14:6-7: *"I am the way and the truth and the life. No one comes to the Father except through me. If you really knew me, you would know my Father as well. From now on, you do know him and have seen him."* With a repentant heart and childlike faith in God's power to change him, the old fisherman humbly answered God's calling: He committed his life to knowing Jesus by heart.

Through God's transformational power the fisherman became like Jesus, and by doing so he touched the very heart of God — and the heart of his own son.

When your children, your spouse, your friends — or even total strangers — come in contact with you, are they in the presence of Jesus? Are they drawn to Him through you? Do they come to know His heart because of yours? If they were actually to meet Jesus on the street, would they sense they already know Him because they know you? If not, why not? And do you have the courage to ask God to change that?

The question that has baffled so many Christians — "What would God

have me do with my life now that I've repented of my sins and trusted Jesus?" — has been answered. You have been placed on this earth to become like Jesus so that others may know Him — by heart. Any other goal or accomplishment in your life should grow out of this purpose.

Sadly, even the church has often misunderstood this truth. Many Christians are being fused into the activities and ministries of the church without the vital internal transformation that makes external expressions of faith the natural fruit of a desire to glorify God. It's time to get beyond the hand clapping of external activities to the very heart of the matter. And that requires that with a repentant heart you trust in God to change dramatically what you could never change yourself. Spiritual transformation does not emerge from your own efforts.

> **Spiritual transformation is God's work of changing a believer into the likeness of Jesus by creating a new identity in Christ and by empowering a lifelong relationship of love, trust, and obedience to glorify God.**

To put it simply, Jesus is the Way to a transformed life. When Jesus begins living out His life through you, He changes everything — and your view of everyone you meet. God will use your transformed heart to forever change your children, your spouse, your friends — even strangers on the street. Just as He used the old fisherman, He will use you to point the way to His Son — so that when others think of you, they will think of Jesus.

That's what happens when you know Jesus by heart.

Week 1
The Heart of Your Faith

Every barrier has been removed between you and knowing God.

Ray walked into his first meeting of Alcoholics Anonymous. Stretched across the front of the room was a sign that read, *"But for the grace of God ...."* He asked the man sitting beside him what the sign meant.

"That depends on your perspective, son," the man replied. "Someone who hasn't been in our shape looks at that sign and us sitting here and completes it, *'But for the grace of God, I'd be one of them.'* That translation used to make me think God gave some people grace and withheld it from others. But one day, as I was reading the Bible, I saw how Jesus cared for those people others avoided — people like you and me. I came to know Jesus personally, like I would a close friend. Now I read that sign, *'Because of the grace of God, Jesus became one of us.'* That perspective makes all the difference in the world."[2]

Think about that for a moment: Jesus became one of us. *One of us.* As unlovable and unworthy as we are, God made the ultimate sacrifice and came to us in Jesus so that we might truly know Him. He didn't shun us; God became one of us. What an amazing truth! That means to know Jesus is to know the heart of God.

Isn't that what you thirst for? What your spirit longs for? *To know the heart of God.* Maybe you've even tried to fill that deep sense of longing in your own way. (You wouldn't be the first to do so.) The Israelites tried to create a relationship with God their own way, too. But they failed miserably: *"We look for light, but all is darkness; for brightness, but we walk in deep shadows. Like the blind we grope along the wall, feeling our way like men without eyes"* (Isa. 59:9b-10a).

You, too, may often feel as if you're blindly groping your way to God. But it doesn't have to be that way. The simple reality is you come to know God only as you enter into a personal relationship with His Son Jesus Christ. Looking in any other direction — stumbling in the dark down any other path — is only to limit what it means to know God. Jesus is the only way to a relationship with God. And only Jesus can remove the huge obstacle that keeps you from God. That obstacle is your sin.

Stop now and ask yourself this crucial question: "Have I come to the

*"But when he, the Spirit of truth, comes, he will guide you into all truth. He will not speak on his own; he will speak only what he hears, and he will tell you what is yet to come. He will bring glory to me by taking what is mine and making it known to you. All that belongs to the Father is mine. That is why I said the Spirit will take what is mine and make it known to you"
(John 16:13-15).*

point in my life where I've realized that Jesus is the only way to remove the sin barrier between God and me?"

The Bible makes it clear in Romans 3:23: *"For all have sinned and come short of the glory of God"* (KJV). The word *sin* means to fall short of a target. It is the failure of a person to live the life which God has planned for him to live. The sin in your life represents a humanly insurmountable barrier between you and God.

And the price of that sin is high. The Bible says, *"The wages of sin is death, but the gift of God is eternal life in Christ Jesus our Lord"* (Rom. 6:23). If you live without God in this life, you will pay the awful price of an eternity separated from Him — because God cannot allow rebellious, sinful people to enter into heaven, the eternal dwelling where He lives in perfect harmony with His people.

But God has such a great love for you — in spite of your rebellion against Him — that He wants to remove the sin that separates you from Him. The fact remains, however, that because of God's righteousness, you — or someone else acceptable to God — must pay the penalty for your sin. So God made the ultimate sacrifice. He sent His one and only Son, Jesus, sinless and pure, to die as a sacrificial lamb for your sins. Romans 5:8 tells you, *"But God demonstrates his own love for us in this: While we were still sinners, Christ died for us."*

The death of Jesus is the greatest demonstration of God's love for you. It is a great love for someone to die in place of a loved one. But Jesus died for those in rebellion — for those who did not love Him in return. The awesome beauty of this sacrificial love is captured in John 3:16: *"For God so loved the world that he gave his one and only Son that whoever believes in him shall not perish but have eternal life."*

How do you receive this gift of sacrificial love and have your sins completely taken away? The Bible says, *"Repent then, and turn to God, so that your sins may be wiped out, that times of refreshing may come from the Lord"* (Acts 3:19). The word *repent* means to turn around and go in a different direction. It means a change of mind and life toward God. If you are willing to turn to God, then God will establish a relationship with you. Your part is to confess your sin and repent; God's part is to forgive you and give you a new identity. That means salvation is not something that you can personally create. It must be a pure act of faith by grace. *Grace* refers to the kindness and love of God in His willingness to forgive and save you. *Faith* means to trust to a point of commitment. You cannot just believe in God. You must be willing to receive God's forgiveness and follow Him. Salvation is God's gift. Ephesians 2:8 explains it this way, *"For it is by grace you have been saved, through faith — and this not from yourselves, it is the gift of God — not by works, so that no one can boast."*

It may be that you now stand with your face pressed hard against the barrier that separates you from the God who loves you so much. If you want God to remove that barrier, Romans 10:9 shows you the way: *"If you confess with your mouth, 'Jesus is Lord,' and believe in your heart that God raised him from the dead, you will be saved."* The word *confess* means to acknowledge to God that Jesus is Lord and Savior — to believe with all your heart that Jesus died on the cross for you and rose from the grave. You must believe that He is alive and that He will change your life through a personal relationship with Him as you follow and obey His teachings.

The Bible says, *"Everyone who calls on the name of the Lord will be saved"* (Rom. 10:13). Anyone can ask God for forgiveness of sin and turn from sin and follow Jesus. If you are choosing to do that, pray a prayer similar to this one:

> **"Lord Jesus,
> I know I am a sinner and need Your forgiveness. I believe Jesus died to forgive me of my sins. I now turn from my sin, ask You to forgive me, and receive Your offer of eternal life. I trust You as my Savior, and I will follow You as my Lord. Thank You for forgiving me of all my sin. Thank You for my new life."**

If you just prayed this prayer of repentance or have done that at some other time in your life, celebrate! Every barrier that once stood between you and a personal relationship with God has been removed. Think about that. Every barrier is gone! Because God has accepted your repentant heart, nothing stands between you and Him. Absolutely nothing. Now you can know His heart — and through the transforming power of the Holy Spirit become everything He wants you to be (Rom. 12:2; John 16:13-15; 2 Cor. 3:18).

So celebrate! This week you'll learn about the core of your faith and how God will use that core to begin your miraculous transformation — a change of your character, your nature, and your perspective.

And we, who with unveiled faces all reflect the Lord's glory, are being transformed into his likeness with ever-increasing glory, which comes from the Lord, who is the Spirit (2 Cor. 3:18).

Day One: The Heart of God

BY THE BOOK

"Man looks at the outward appearance, but the Lord looks at the heart"
(1 Sam.16:7b).

When understanding the relationship between you and God, there are some things that can only be grasped by talking about the heart. That's a big shift from the world's perspective, which takes stock by adding up a checklist of external accomplishments. But the Bible doesn't hesitate to refer to heart when it is talking about who you really are. In 1 Samuel 16:7b you can see that God has His eye on who you are deep inside, what your values and commitments are — the real you with all masks off. And that is where He wants to connect with you. Repeat the following truth: "God wants to have a heart-to-heart, deeply personal, totally fulfilling relationship with me."

What does that mean? It means you are immensely important to God, and He wants to change the way you respond to Him. Despite a secular song which claims, "God is watching us from a distance," God is not viewing your life from afar. He's right where you are. He's an intimately personal God who wants to pull you close and share His own heart with you so you can know, without a doubt, the depth of His love, His grace, and His mercy.

That kind of relationship may be somewhat difficult to grasp with the mind. But perhaps you've experienced a personal relationship with another individual that has given you a glimpse of what it means to know someone "by heart." List that individual's name below, along with the characteristics that person displayed that gave you the confidence to open your own heart to such a close relationship.

_____

_____

_____

_____

_____

_____

_____

When you truly connect with another person, it's almost as if you share the same heart. A deep "heart love" develops that brings your two spirits into sync. You become as one. That person's pain is your pain. That person's joy is your joy. Separating your two hearts is impossible. Describe a time when you experienced personal pain or joy because the person you mentioned previously experienced those feelings.

_____

_____
_____
_____
_____
_____
_____
_____
_____
_____
_____
_____

In the Book of Philemon you can see a clear example of heart love. Paul came to love Onesimus deeply, a slave who had run away from the household of a man named Philemon. While Paul was in prison, Onesimus ministered to him and became dear to the apostle's heart. Paul sent Onesimus back to Philemon, preceded by written instructions that Philemon receive Onesimus *"no longer as a slave, but better than a slave, as a dear brother. He is very dear to me but even more dear to you, both as a man and as a brother in the Lord"* (Philem. 16).

Paul's appeal was based on Onesimus' having become a believer. The Apostle made it clear that Philemon's response to Onesimus should be the same as if he were responding to Paul himself. He said, *"I am sending him — who is my very heart — back to you"* (Philem. 12).

In a sense God sent a similar — but even stronger — message to Peter, James, and John at a time when they were still trying to comprehend the identity of Jesus and how they should respond to Him.

One day, while standing before the three on a mountaintop, Jesus was transfigured before them. *"His face shone like the sun, and his clothes became as white as the light. Just then there appeared before them Moses and Elijah, talking with Jesus"* (Matt. 17:2b-3).

Peter, enraptured by the scene, offered to put up altars for Moses, Elijah, and Jesus. But at that precise moment God chose to clarify forever who Jesus is and what He means to God in relation to Moses, Elijah — and all mankind for that matter. As Paul had sent a letter to Philemon on papyrus, God also sent a distinct message on the mountaintop: *"A bright cloud enveloped them, and a voice from the cloud said: 'This is my Son, whom I love; with him I am well pleased. Listen to him!' "* (Matt. 17:5).

What a stunning statement! God was stating — then and for all eternity — that Jesus is His very heart. He was telling the world: "Respond to Jesus as you would respond to Me."

In John 14:6-7 Jesus dispels any doubt about His role and how it affects you personally: *"I am the way and the truth and the life. No one comes to the Father except through me. If you really knew me, you would know my father as well. From now on you do know him and have seen him"* (John 14:6-7).

The path to a heart-to-heart relationship with God is through Jesus Christ. There is no other way. Because of the ultimate sacrifice of Jesus, God has accepted your repentant heart, and He wants to begin His work of transforming you into the likeness of His Son. No longer must you wonder: What would God have me do with my life now that I've repented of my sins and put my faith in Jesus? In his book *Just Like Jesus*, Max Lucado gives you the answer: "God loves you just the way you are, but he refuses to leave you that way. He wants you to be just like Jesus."[3]

There is no higher calling.

This Is Your Life: Obstacle Course

List three things in your life today that could hinder the development of a heart-to-heart relationship with God.

_____

_____

_____

What steps will God empower you to take to overcome these obstacles?

_____

_____

_____

_____

_____

_____

_____

_____

Ask a close friend or family member to pray with you for victory over these three areas.

Day Two: Do You Know?

In that stunning moment when Mary held the baby Jesus in her arms for the first time and kissed His soft skin, did she know she was kissing the very face of God? Did she know that — for the first time in history — a mere human was face-to-face, heart-to-heart with the Almighty God?

Every now and then a song is written that drives truth to the window of the universe for every eye to see. Mark Lowry and Buddy Green paint a powerful picture of the identity of Jesus in their song, "Mary, Did You Know?"

> *Mary, did you know your baby boy would someday walk on water?*
> *Mary, did you know your baby boy would save your sons and daughters?*
> *Did you know your baby boy has come to make you new?*
> *This child that you've delivered will soon deliver you.*
> *Mary, did you know?*
>
> *Mary, did you know your baby boy would give sight to a blind man?*
> *Mary, did you know your baby boy would calm a storm with his hand?*
> *Did you know that your baby boy has walked where angels trod?*
> *When you kissed your little baby, you kissed the face of God.*
> *Mary, did you know?*
>
> *Mary, did you know your baby boy is Lord of all creation?*
> *Mary, did you know your baby boy will someday rule the nations?*
> *Did you know your baby boy was Heaven's perfect Lamb?*
> *This sleeping child you're holding is the great I Am.*[4]

Do *you* know? Do you know that Jesus in whom you have placed your faith is truly God who became visible so that you can ultimately know Him (John 1:14)? Do you know that Jesus is "Lord of all creation" (Col.1:15-16)? Do you know that Jesus "is the great I Am"? That His name Immanuel means "God with us" (Matt. 1:22-23)? Whole new boundaries are estab-

BY THE BOOK

"The Word became flesh and made his dwelling among us. We have seen his glory, the glory of the One and only who came from the Father, full of grace and truth" (John 1:14).

He is the image of the invisible God, the firstborn over all creation. For by him all things were created — things in heaven and on earth, visible and invisible, whether thrones or powers or rulers or authorities; all things were created by him and for him (Col. 1:15-16).

"The virgin will be with child and will give birth to a son, and they will call him Immanuel" — which means, "God with us" (Matt. 1:22-23).

lished when you base your commitment to follow Jesus on who He is. You are relating one-to-one with Almighty God Himself, not a mere representative or a "step on the ladder" toward finding God.

Think about it. To know Jesus is to know God. In John 10:30 Jesus makes it dramatically clear: *"I and the Father are one."* Jesus is God in human form (John 1:14). He is the message of hope to the lost world. And He is the key to your spiritual transformation.

In his book *The Way of Holiness*, Stephen Olford pinpoints the ultimate centrality of Jesus with this statement: "The Lord Jesus Christ is totally adequate. It is not Jesus plus; it is Jesus period! Everything is in Jesus, and Jesus is everything!"[5] Olford has summarized what the entire Bible is saying: Jesus is the only way.

In Colossians 1:17-23a, Paul establishes that Jesus is central to all things. Paul uses the word *image*, which means far more than what some might claim to be true of Jesus. He is not a light from a distant star that lets you know what a star is like. He is not heat from a stove that warns you of what you can expect if you touch the stove. He is not merely representative of God, showing you what God is like should you ever meet Him face-to-face. Jesus is God. To know Jesus is to come face-to-face, heart-to-heart with God Himself.

Basing your life on Jesus as central to all things necessitates a radical re-ordering of your goals, your ambitions, and how you relate to others. Paul summarized his own radically transformed life, which placed Jesus at the core, this way: *"I have been crucified with Christ and I no longer live, but Christ lives in me. The life I live in the body, I live by faith in the Son of God, who loved me and gave himself for me"* (Gal. 2:20).

About now you may be saying, "I'm no apostle Paul! How could I ever transform my life to be like Jesus?"

You can't. But God can. He is the key to your transformation — not you. It is the Spirit of God using the Word of God that convicts you of your sin and convinces you to repent. With repentance you choose to turn from a life of sin, but it is God who effects the turning, not you. He is the Author and Implementor of transformation. Paul's change from persecutor to evangelist dramatically proves what can happen when a person turns from sin and allows God to turn life around. You see, a transformed life is not simply attained by mimicking the actions of Jesus. Like the old fisherman mentioned in the opening segment of your study, and like the apostle Paul, you must humbly ask God to change you from the inside out so that Christ is formed in you, so that your hearts beat as one (Gal. 4:19). True spiritual transformation requires a repentant heart and a faithful understanding and allegiance to Jesus' statement *"apart from me you can do nothing"* (John 15:5b). Paul knew that. The old fisherman knew that. Do you know that?

Stop right now and ask God to dispel any belief you might have that spiritual transformation is impossible. Lay your life before Him and humbly ask Him to change you from the inside out. Acknowledge that there is nothing you can do to make this change happen. All God requires from you is a repentant, faithful heart. He will do the rest. He did it with Paul. He did it with the old fisherman. He will begin a miracle within you too. After all, He's in the miracle business.

This Is Your Life: A New Perspective

Basing your life on Jesus as central to all things requires a radical shift. How have you viewed Jesus in the past?

_____

_____

_____

_____

_____

What areas of your life will this shift in perspective affect the most?

_____

_____

_____

_____

_____

_____

My dear children, for who I am again in the pains of childbirth until Christ is formed in you (Gal. 4:19).

THE MAIN THING

The Lord Jesus is totally adequate. It is Jesus. Period.

CHECK POINT

What scares you about getting to know a new person?

_____

_____

_____

What scares you about getting to know God more intimately?

_____

_____

_____

Ask God to work in your life to dispel these fears.

Day Three: Your Personal Miracle

By the Book

"If you love me, you will obey what I command. And I will ask the Father and he will give you another Counselor to be with you forever — the Spirit of truth. The world cannot accept him, because it neither sees him nor knows him. But you know him for he lives with you and will be in you"
(John 14:15-17).

The teachers of the law and the Pharisees brought in a woman caught in adultery. They made her stand before the group and said to Jesus, "Teacher, this woman was caught in the act of adultery. In the Law Moses commanded us to stone such a woman. Now what do you say?" They were using this question as a trap, in order to have a basis for accusing him. But

Jim Sloan is a walking miracle. All of his coworkers are amazed that he treats everyone with respect and kindness. Why the amazement? This is Jim's second time around at the production plant where he works. The first time was quite different. That tenure was wasted by his disrespect and blatant abuse of other people and the company's rules.

But the story actually begins years before when Jim was involved in the accidental and senseless death of a fellow college student. Though never actually charged with manslaughter, Jim lived with gut-wrenching guilt about his friend's death. The guilt was so gripping that he tried to numb it with alcohol and cover it with an abusive temper. Not only was he abusive at work, he was also cruel to his wife and children. Eventually he lost both his job and his family.

One day, as Jim stood alone in the echoing house that had once been a home, the door bell rang. When he opened the door, Jim recognized a familiar face but could not place who the woman was. She identified herself as the mother of the young man who had died. She went on to explain that the reason she was there was because of her new-found faith in Jesus Christ. Jim listened intently as she explained the hatred and bitterness she had lived with for years because of her son's death. But because God had forgiven her of all her sins and changed her heart, she had come seeking Jim's forgiveness for all the hatred she had felt toward him. She also came giving Jim forgiveness for the role he played in her son's death.

Stunned by her message, Jim asked the woman to tell him more about her new-found faith and how Jesus had given her the capacity to forgive. The woman told him that God loved her and Jim so much that He had sent Jesus, His sinless Son, to pay the price for their sins by dying on the cross. The acute awareness of that kind of sacrificial love and the evidence of its power in the mother's life, brought Jim to his knees. For the very first time in his life, Jim found the freedom to be what he could never be before because of his past. He asked God to forgive him for causing the death of the woman's son and for all of the other wrong things he had done. Jim laid the shambles of the first half of his life at the foot of the cross and asked God to show him how to live the rest of his life for God's glory.

No longer was Jim a man weighed down by guilt and anger. He was a child of the forgiving God, a man with a Lord, a man with a new heart — a heart like that of Jesus. And from that moment on, through the transforming power of the Holy Spirit, Jim was never the same. Daily, God was changing Jim from the inside out (John 14:15-17). And everyone Jim came in contact with could see the difference.[6]

Jim and this forgiving mother are not alone in receiving freedom to become what they never could be before their repentance. In John 8:3-11 a woman caught in adultery was brought before Jesus by the Pharisees. How utterly alone and scared this woman must have felt as she was dragged by a mob of pious men to what she was sure would be her painful death.

But the response of Jesus was amazing. Rather than condemn her, Jesus told the woman's accusers to throw the first stone if they were without sin. Can't you just see the heads-down-foot-shuffling that was going on after Jesus made *that* statement! There was probably a lot of dust being kicked around, but no stones were thrown. Eventually, one by one, her accusers walked away. They didn't have an innocent leg to stand on. They knew it. And Jesus knew it.

As that woman stood alone before Jesus she, too, looked into forgiving eyes and — for the very first time in her life — embraced the freedom to be what she never could be before because of her past. She was brought to Jesus as one accused. But she surrendered to Him with a broken, contrite heart. And in His amazing grace, Jesus gave her forgiveness and the power to begin again. Imagine how this woman must have felt! Can't you just see her — running home with her spirit soaring! Tears of joy streaming down her face. Free at last to begin again. Free at last. The personal miracle of spiritual healing can never be overstated.

You, too, are a miracle. With Jesus' forgiveness and a new heart like His, you can finally be what you could never be without Him. That reality of Christ in you has already begun to transform your life. You now are intended to be Christ's mirror image. Paul wrote many times about the miraculous transformation of his own life. He sums it up in Colossians 1:27: *"To them God has chosen to make known among the Gentiles the glorious riches of this mystery, which is Christ in you, the hope of glory."*

Your personal miracle is an unmerited blessing from God. It frees you to be what you never could be before God touched you — *to be just like Jesus* — whose main reason for living was to glorify God with every breath and every step He took.

In tomorrow's lesson you will learn how dramatically changed you really are. But right now, stop and thank God for forgiving you of all the sins you have committed. Thank Him for healing you spiritually. Thank Him for giv-

Jesus bent down and started to write on the ground with his finger. When they kept on questioning him, he straightened up and said to them, "If anyone is without sin, let him be the first to throw a stone at her." Again he stooped down and wrote on the ground. At this, those who heard began to go away one at a time, the older ones first, until only Jesus was left with the woman still standing there. Jesus straightened up and asked her, "Woman, where are they? Has no one condemned you?" "No one, sir," she said. "Then neither do I condemn you," Jesus declared. "Go now and leave your life of sin" (John 8:3-11).

ing you the freedom and the power to be everything He wants you to be. You truly are a miracle of love and grace.

This Is Your Life: *No Stones to Throw*

It took a miracle of love and grace to change you from a lost sinner to a child of God. Do you bring the gift of forgiveness and grace to others, just as it has been brought to you by Jesus? Think of someone whom you hold a grudge against — or someone you perceive holds a grudge against you. Write that person's name below.

_____

Did you throw verbal stones at that person — or did you offer forgiveness and grace? Remember, none of us has an innocent leg to stand on. If you threw stones at the person you listed above, ask God to give you the humble strength to contact that individual (in person, or via a phone call or letter) and ask for forgiveness. Use the time as an opportunity to explain the miracle of love and grace that enables you to drop your stones and forgive just as Jesus forgave you. Record the results of your contact.

_____
_____
_____
_____
_____
_____

CHECK POINT

What personal problem have you recently tried to solve on your own that you need to bring to God today? Describe that problem, and give it to Him in prayer. Then watch God work.

_____
_____
_____
_____
_____
_____
_____

Day Four: Your New Spiritual DNA

Every person's DNA (deoxyribonucleic acid) is different — except that of identical twins. For them, their perfectly matched internal coding makes them one and the same. Their very hearts, their very cells are created as one at conception; they are mirror reflections of one another — inside and out.

You may not have an identical twin, but the second you repented of your sins and God accepted you as His forgiven child, you were reborn. Immediately God gave you your birthright — a new spiritual DNA (1 Pet. 1:3b-4). And guess what? Your spiritual DNA is a perfect match of that of God's Son, Jesus Christ. When God accepted you as His own, He changed everything about you (2 Cor. 5:17).

Stop for a moment and rewind your mental tape back to the time when you asked God to forgive you of your sins and He accepted your repentant heart. Describe where you were.

_____

_____

Now, close your eyes and see yourself at that spot. Maybe it was at the altar of your church. Maybe it was at the foot of your bed. Maybe it was in a Sunday School classroom. Wherever it was, pull that picture up. Got it? Now rewind back a few frames to the second *before* you repented and embraced God's salvation, *before* He accepted you as His forgiven child. Freeze-frame right there. See that person? Through the miraculous work of a God whose amazing love transcends — and transforms — you are not now who you were in that mental picture.

When you became a child of God, you became an entirely new person — with an entirely new lease on life. Just as God gives a newborn baby all the DNA code needed to grow to adulthood, He immediately gave you the new spiritual DNA you needed to live a life that glorifies Him, everything you need to walk with God and live a life of love, trust, and obedience — just like Jesus did. As a newborn believer, God has given you the spiritual DNA that you need to grow to spiritual maturity. Thus, as you grow, you are becoming who you already are in Christ. That means that as a child of God you now have a heart like His Son Jesus.

Think about that. You have been given a second chance at life — a second chance to change the world. And with Jesus empowering you, you can do it. Why? Because you are in Jesus and Jesus is in you (John 14:20). Because

He has given us new birth into a living hope through the resurrection of Jesus Christ from the dead, and into an inheritance that can never perish, spoil or fade — kept for you in heaven (1 Pet. 1:3b-4).

Therefore, if anyone is in Christ, is he a new creation; the old has gone, the new has come (2 Cor. 5:17).

"On that day you will realize that I am in my Father, and you are in me, and I am in you" (John 14:20).

You were taught, with regard to your former way of life, to put off your old self, which is being corrupted by its deceitful desires; to be made new in the attitude of your minds; and to put on the new self, created to be like God in true righteousness and holiness (Eph. 4:22-23).

He is in you and you are in Him you can do what He has done — bring glory to God with every step you take. You may have the same physical body, but His Spirit now lives in you. In John 3:5-6 Jesus explains it this way: *"I tell you the truth, no one can enter the kingdom of God unless he is born of water and the Spirit. Flesh gives birth to flesh, but the Spirit gives birth to spirit."* Because the Spirit of Jesus now lives in you, you have the ability — and the calling — to glorify God on the outside with every step you take, just as Jesus did (Eph. 4:22-23). Stop for a moment and retrace your spiritual path:

Step One: God changed you. The old you has been transformed. *"Therefore if any man be in Christ, he is a new creature: old things are passed away; behold, all things are become new"* (2 Cor. 5:17).

Step Two: God gave you a new spiritual identity in Christ. You now have Christ in you and you are in Him (John 14:20). *"To them God has chosen to make known among the Gentiles the glorious riches of this mystery, which is Christ in you, the hope of glory"* (Col. 1:27).

Step Three: God will use your life for His glory. Through your heart-to-heart relationship with Jesus, God has empowered you to love, trust, and obey Him. God's love and power will be revealed to others through your surrendered life. Other people will see Jesus in you. And God will be glorified because of it (John 13:31b; 17:26).

You are God's cherished child by rebirth, safe and loved — just like His Son Jesus. Have no fear. You are loved unconditionally. Jesus will live out His life through your surrendered life. And the world will be a better place because of it (Phil. 1:6-7a, 8-11).

This Is Your Life: Time for a Change

List some areas of your life God is changing through His Spirit living in you.

_____
_____
_____
_____
_____
_____
_____
_____
_____

How will God use those changes for His glory?

_____
_____
_____
_____
_____
_____

filled with the fruit of righteousness that comes through Jesus Christ—to the glory and praise of God" (Phil. 1:6-7a,8-11).

THE MAIN THING

God has radically changed you from within; you have everything you need to glorify God with your life.

CHECK POINT

Think of one thing you can do today that will help someone else know your heart. Write it here. Then do it.

_____
_____
_____
_____
_____
_____
_____

Day Five: Your New Vision

BY THE BOOK

Therefore we do not lose heart. Though outwardly we are wasting away, yet inwardly we are being renewed day by day. For our light and momentary troubles are achieving for us an eternal glory that far outweighs them all. So we fix our eyes not on what is seen, but on what is unseen. For what is seen is temporary, but what is unseen is eternal (2 Cor. 4:16-18).

A copy of an ancient letter tells the following story: The coliseum was packed, the crowd thirsty for blood. Several men and women were roughly herded into the center of the arena. One sympathetic guard whispered to the trembling group: "Lions seldom attack people who remain tightly grouped together."

Suddenly, four intentionally starved lions sprang from their opened cages and began circling their prey. The group of Christians huddled more tightly together. But as a huge lion approached one side, a young pregnant woman stumbled and fell forward. The lion immediately pounced, dragging the young woman and her unborn child to a gruesome death.

Even in the face of this unspeakable horror, those Christians who remained carefully sank to their knees, lifted their faces to heaven, and began to sing a song of faith and hope, a song that expressed the same message of one that was to be written and sung centuries later by another Christian facing earthly torment: *"Be thou my vision, O Lord of my heart ..."*

As their voices rose to the ears of the Roman general in charge of the event, he solemnly asked a question of no one in particular: "How is it that these Christians can look into the very abyss of death and yet sing songs of faith and hope?"

A young soldier named Adrianis who had, unknown to the general and others in the coliseum become a Christian himself while working in the Christian-filled dungeons, answered quietly, "They say, sir, that it is because of unseen things that they see."[7]

The gift of unseen things. What did those huddled Christians see that the masses craving blood did not? They saw eternity — the vision that is planted in the heart of every Christian, the vision that sustains, the vision that makes all the difference in this world — and eternity beyond. Even when the eyes of the Christians huddled in the center of that coliseum saw torture and death all around them, their hearts saw God's eternal purposes as greater than their immediate needs and circumstances. Their eternal vision told them that even if their earthly fates mirrored that of the young pregnant woman, death in the coliseum did not signal the end. They had eternity in their hearts. And upon seeing and hearing the expression of that eternal vision, the stone heart of a Roman general was softened.

Stop for a moment. Close your eyes. Can you see yourself in a world gone mad, a world under the grip of a New-Millennium Hitler? What would you do if certain death snarled in your face? Would you sing a song of faith and hope as the coliseum Christians did?

"No! I wouldn't be able to sing!" you say. "I'd be scared speechless!"

No doubt, as the lions circled the coliseum Christians were scared, too. But think about it. Because Jesus lives in you, because you have His spiritual heritage, you possess that same vision of eternity that sustained the early Christians — even in the midst of indescribable pain and anguish. That vision of eternity is part of your inheritance in Christ. You cannot separate yourself from it; it is woven into the very fabric of your being.

The apostle Paul clearly explains the gift of the unseen in 2 Corinthians 4:16-18. His words indicate that even when we are at the end of our rope, we are never at the end of hope. *The Message* paraphrases it this way: *"We're not giving up.... There's far more here than meets the eye."* In John 14:19 Jesus paints this picture of the vision: *"Before long, the world will not see me anymore, but you will see me. Because I live, you also will live."* This eternal vision remains unseen to those who live their lives without Jesus because they do not have the heart to grasp it.

Think of someone you know whose life — even in the midst of intense struggle — mirrors this keen vision of eternity, someone you believe would, just like the coliseum Christians, sing a song of faith and hope, even when facing death. Write that person's name, along with the "coliseum" characteristics he or she possesses.

_____

_____

_____

_____

_____

Now take a self-assessment. What qualities has God planted in your own life that indicate your own vision for eternity? List them.

_____

_____

_____

_____

_____

_____

Still think you don't have the kind of vision it takes to stare death in

Christians hold in their hearts a vision of certainty and hope that those without Jesus can never know.

the face and sing like the coliseum Christians did? Then ask yourself these questions: Are you completely satisfied with earthly pleasures and pursuits? Are they really enough for you? Or do you have an almost indescribable longing, a yearning for things to be different, a hungering desire for fairness to reign, a thirst you can't quite quench no matter how hard you try? That yearning, that unquenchable thirst is evidence of the vision of eternity God has planted in your own heart. It is the proof that you, too, have your vision of the unseen.

With your rebirth in Christ, God gave you a glimpse of perfection. But it is only a glimpse. You cannot see into the future or comprehend everything God has for you in eternity. But you know in your heart it is where you belong, where you ultimately long to be. You are created in His perfect image and you can never be completely satisfied on this earth because you have a spiritual thirst; you have eternal value — and nothing but the eternal God and His perfect rule can truly satisfy you. Ecclesiastes 3:11 says it beautifully: *"God has made everything beautiful in its time. He has also set eternity in the hearts of men; yet they cannot fathom what God has done from beginning to end."*

The vision for eternity that God wove into your soul the day He accepted your repentant heart is the faith that will see you through to the end — no matter what that earthly end may be. Such visionary faith shone in the life of seminary professor Oscar Thompson — even as cancer ravaged his body. When asked by a friend how he could still smile even though the excruciating pain seared him, Oscar replied, "I have learned our lives are crucified between two thieves — yesterday and tomorrow. By God's grace I will not surrender to those thieves but will live today — for I've also learned that God doesn't give dying grace on a non-dying day." With a vision that saw beyond his pain, Oscar Thompson continued to smile and live a life that glorified God until the day God took him home.

It is visionary faith like that of Oscar Thompson that will enable you to walk day-by-day to glorify God. That kind of visionary faith is what God will use to transform you to be like Jesus. It is that kind of faith that will move mountains in your life. It is that kind of faith that will draw others to Jesus through you. And when life is pulling you down, it is that kind of faith, that kind of vision, that will enable you to look up. And sing . . .

> *Be Thou my vision, O Lord of my heart;*
> > *Naught be all else to me, save that Thou art:*
> *Thou my best thought, by day or by night,*
> > *Waking or sleeping, Thy presence my light.*

Be Thou my wisdom, and Thou my true word;
*   I ever with Thee and Thou with me, Lord:*
Thou my great Father, I Thy true son,
*   Thou in me dwelling, and I with Thee one.*

Riches I heed not, or man's empty praise,
*   Thou mine inheritance, now and always:*
Thou and Thou only, first in my heart,
*   High King of heaven, my treasure Thou art.*

High King of heaven, my victory won,
*   May I reach heaven's joys, O bright heav'n's Sun!*
Heart of my own heart, whatever befall,
*   Still be my vision, O Ruler of all.*[8]

This Is Your Life: Visionary Living

Describe a time in your life when your faith, your God-given vision for eternity, sustained you through a great difficulty.

_____

_____

How would you have handled the crisis if you hadn't been a Christian?

_____

_____

Think of someone you know who is not a Christian but is going through a difficult time in his or her life. Write that individual's name.

_____

What can you do this week that will help that person see the vision of the eternal that you have in your heart, the vision that helps you sing when lions roar?

_____

_____

CHECK POINT

On *Day Four* of this week, you were challenged to do something that would enable another person to better know your heart. Describe what you did and the results of your effort.

_____

_____

_____

_____

_____

_____

_____

_____

_____

_____

_____

_____

_____

_____

_____

_____

_____

_____

_____

A Moment with Jesus

Jesus never spoke of anything that did not come from God. He delivered God's message with ultimate authority. Listen to what Jesus says in John 12:47-50.

"As for the person who hears my words but does not keep them, I do not judge him. For I did not come to judge the world, but to save it. There is a judge for the one who rejects me and does not accept my words; that very word which I spoke will condemn him at the last day. For I did not speak of my own accord, but the Father who sent me commanded me what to say and how to say it. I know that his command leads to eternal life. So whatever I say is just what the Father has told me to say."

Jesus made it clear that His words carried the ultimate weight. Jesus spoke and lived with perfect authority, because God Himself was directing every word He spoke and every action He took.

There's a high price to pay when you ignore the Voice of Authority. In the Sermon on the Mount Jesus warned, *"But everyone who hears these words of mine and does not put them into practice is like a foolish man who built his house on sand. The rain came down, the streams rose, and the winds blew and beat against that house, and it fell with a great crash"* (Matt. 7:26-27).

Jesus made it clear that to live by His Word is the main foundation of life. To build a life on any other religion, philosophy, or teaching will result in a brutal crash. The people Jesus spoke to as He delivered the Sermon on the Mount recognized His clout. They *"were amazed at his teachings, because he taught as one who had authority, and not as the teachers of the law"* (Matt. 7:28b-29).

It's no wonder that Jesus said, *"I am the way and the truth and the life. No one comes to the Father except through me"* (John 14:6). Jesus was the voice of God then, and He is the voice of God now. Are you listening to what He is saying?

Jesus Spoke with Authority

"And in Closing ..."

As you come to the close of this week's study, spend a few minutes reviewing the lessons.

What do you believe is the most important thing God has taught you this week?

_____

_____

_____

_____

What do you believe is the main action God would have you take based upon this week's study?

_____

_____

_____

_____

Spend some time in prayer. Thank God for speaking to you through your study and ask Him to help you put into life practice what you are learning.

Week 2
Your Transformed Heart

Michael Plant, an experienced yachtsman piloting a superior vessel, set out to cross the Atlantic Ocean. This highly skilled man, who had previously navigated many severe storms, sailed into a typical summer squall. Days later a freighter near the Portuguese Azores found Plant's boat floating upside down. Michael Plant's body was never found.

The mystery of why such an experienced sailor did not survive a storm much milder than those he had previously faced bewildered investigators. Plant's magnificent boat was built to plow through storms much rougher than the one he had encountered, yet the boat capsized. Investigators soon discovered why. An 8,000-pound keel weight had broken loose during the storm. To remain stable, a boat must have more weight below the waterline than above. Once the balance was gone, Plant's magnificent boat capsized and he perished.[9]

The importance of having more weight beneath the waterline than above it can be applied to your life. There is a danger in giving attention to the outward activities of spiritual life while neglecting the inner transformation of the heart that comes from an intimate relationship with Jesus. Don't misunderstand. Jesus wants to accomplish a great deal through you for God's glory. He wants you to be active in the ministries of your church, to actively fulfill the Great Commission. But He wants you to be a secure vessel; otherwise, you might find yourself floating upside down in stormy seas. When temptations, tough circumstances, and threats to your faith bombard you, you are in grave danger if there is more outward spiritual activity in your life than inward, intimate, spiritual relationship with Jesus.

Last week you focused on the core of your faith, Jesus Christ, and how your miraculous new identity in Him gives you His spiritual DNA and a new vision for eternity that the unbeliever does not possess. This week you will see how God takes your forgiven, forever-changed heart and transforms your entire being into one that will stand the test of any storm — because it is the likeness of Jesus Himself. But first, you'll take a look at the exhausting detours many Christians take when they try to take transformation into their own hands.

There is a danger of giving attention to the outward activities of spiritual life while neglecting the inner transformation of the heart that comes from an intimate relationship with Jesus.

WEEK 2 AT A GLANCE

Day 1
Detours of the Heart

Day 2
Jesus, the Change Maker

Day 3
What's Love Got to Do with It?

Day 4:
Trust and Obey

Day 5
The Glory Shines Through

Day One: Detours of the Heart

BY THE BOOK

The Sovereign Lord has given me an instructed tongue to know the word that sustains the weary. He wakens me morning by morning, wakens my ear to listen like one being taught. The Sovereign Lord has opened my ears, and I have not been rebellious; I have not drawn back (Isa. 50:4-5).

Very early in the morning, while it was still dark, Jesus got up, left the house and went off to a solitary place, where he prayed (Mark 1:35).

So Jesus often withdrew to lonely places and prayed (Luke 5:16).

When you've been away from home, a warm, wonderful feeling envelops you as you walk through your door. All around you are those familiar aromas that let you know you are home — safe and wrapped in the love of your family.

When Jesus accepted your repentant heart, He opened the door to His own heart and said, "Welcome home." He invited you to spend time with Him, to get to know Him. And you really wanted that.

But then the doorbell buzzed, the phone rang, the personal appeals came, and you were compelled to run out the door — to get busy doing the things Christians are supposed to do. You became a Christian on the move. Places to go. Things to do. People to see . . . .

But as you're zipping through your life, don't you often hear the soft inner voice saying, "Come home..."? That voice is your very heart — the heart of Jesus — calling you to spend time with Him (Is. 50:4-5). But it seems there is so little time to do everything that needs to be done. So you pedal just a little harder, a little faster, to accomplish your "spiritual goals" — although, oddly enough, there's a great disparity between your efforts and the results. And you're bone-tired. "What is wrong?" you wonder. "Shouldn't I be energized by serving God?"

The truth is, you need to stop what you're doing and listen to your heart. Remember, Jesus is your life — your heartbeat. His life is with you; your life is with Him. To be truly transformed means to be conscious of Jesus living in you and you living in Jesus every moment of every day. That oneness requires a daily, minute-by-minute growing relationship with Jesus.

Think about it. You've been going full tilt for a long time, actively participating in the outward expressions of spiritual life. But you've neglected the inner transformation that comes from an intimate relationship with Jesus. Like a boat that has more weight on the surface than below the waterline, you're out of balance, in grave danger of capsizing.

"Not me," you say?

Let's see. List the spiritual activities you are currently involved in and the amount of time you commit to each one in a typical week. These can be things such as teaching Sunday School, working in the church's sound booth, serving on the church building committee, or working in the neighborhood soup kitchen.

_____
_____
_____
_____
_____

Now, write the amount of time you spend in an average week in solitude with God, developing your personal relationship with Him. _____

Do you think you might be a bit out of balance? If so, it's time to go home. Jesus is waiting there for you with the secret to the spiritually transformed life. He revealed it in John 15:5b: *"Apart from me you can do nothing."*

All of the activities you listed are, most likely, worthwhile ministries. It's just that the scales are tipped the wrong way. There must be priority time set aside to spend in your personal relationship with Jesus.

Jesus understood His lifeline connection to His Father, and He made Himself at home in His Father's love. That means He daily prepared His heart to commune with His loving Father because His Father was the Source of His strength, His power, and His wisdom. Notice the many times in Scripture where Jesus pulled away from doing to be with His Father — to be loved by God, nurtured by God, empowered by God, and guided by God (Mark 1:35; Luke 5:16; 6:12). Jesus knew how vital that time alone with His Father was to His ministry on earth. Jesus knew what to say and do each day (and what not to do) because He spent time in solitary prayer with His Heavenly Father — His Guiding Light. Did the earthly ministry of Jesus suffer because of the time He spent away from others in solitude with God? Absolutely not. His ministry was empowered by it.

Think about it this way. When you're at home, the real you comes shining though. That's the person Jesus wants to work with. Spiritual transformation means that day by day, Jesus takes that real you — your character, your nature, your perspective — and forever changes you into another form — His form. It's a progressive change of "inward essence" rather than a sudden transition from one lifestyle to another. It's not outward activity; it's a "forming" of Christ in you (Gal. 4:19). In Romans 12:2 Paul makes it clear that this transformation is God's work — not yours. It is a guided process rather than a self-directed push.

Of course, it's easy in today's "to-do list" evangelical culture to become focused on the fruit of your efforts rather than on the Source that makes fruit possible. Even the church often unwittingly promotes activity-based

Now it came to pass in those days that He went out to a mountain to pray, and continued all night in prayer to God (Luke 6:12, NKJV).

My dear children, for whom I am again in the pains of childbirth until Christ is formed in you (Gal. 4:19).

Do not conform any longer to the pattern of this world, but be transformed by the renewing of your mind. Then you will be able to test and approve what God's will is — his good, pleasing, and perfect will (Rom. 12:2).

"I am the vine; you are the branches. If a man remains in me and I in him, he will bear much fruit; apart from me you can do nothing" (John 15:5).

THE MAIN THING

The secret to the transformed life is a daily internal nurturing of your relationship with Jesus, not the completion of an outward "to-do list for Jesus."

CHECK POINT

Talk with someone you know who has an identical twin. Ask that person to describe the unique bond he or she shares with that twin. Then think about the unique bond you have with Jesus because He lives in you. List ways that your bond with Christ empowers you to do things you thought you could never do.

_____

_____

_____

_____

Christianity. But the question that emerges from Jesus' teaching of the relationship between the Vine and the branches in John 15:5 is simple and direct: Is your personal relationship with Jesus closer today than it was this time last month?

Jesus didn't worry about producing fruit; fruit appeared wherever He was because of Whose He was — not because of what He did. By making it your priority to become more like Jesus, you, too, will bear fruit naturally. If you're not more like Jesus today than you were this time last month, it's time for your life to change.

This Is Your Life: A Not-to-Do List

To make more time for developing your personal relationship with Jesus, list some activities, hobbies, pastimes, or other endeavors you can cut back on or discontinue (either temporarily or permanently) so that you can dedicate that time to God's work of spiritual transformation. What about your television viewing habits? What about cruising the Internet for hours on end with no place in particular to go? Newspaper reading habits? Computer games? You can probably come up with a bucketful of daily habits that could free plenty of time for your personal spiritual growth. By reordering the time you give to such things each day, you're taking a giant step toward the balanced life, a giant step toward being transformed into the likeness of Jesus.

_____

_____

_____

_____

_____

What steps can you take that will safeguard your time of solitude with God?

_____

_____

_____

_____

_____

_____

_____

Day Two: Jesus, the Change Maker

BY THE BOOK

To this you were called, because Christ suffered for you, leaving you an example, that you should follow in his steps (1 Pet. 2:21).

Mary had a tough time in elementary school. Born with a cleft lip, she was very self-conscious. The other children constantly told her that she was ugly and different. But one bright spot in Mary's life was her teacher. She was tall, slender, and pretty. Mary often dreamed of being like her.

Each year the teacher would administer a hearing test for all of the children. The procedure was called the "whisper test." Each child would be asked to step outside the classroom and place his or her ear to the door while the teacher would whisper something. The results were simple: If the child could recite back to the teacher what was said, the child passed the test.

When it was Mary's turn to take the test she heard seven words that changed her life forever. The teacher whispered: "I wish you were my little girl."[10]

With just such a whisper, Jesus changed every person He ever met on earth. No, they didn't all heed His ultimate call; but each person was forever changed. Think about the rich man who asked Jesus, *"What good thing must I do to get eternal life?"* (Matt. 19:16b). Jesus told him to sell everything he owned, give it to the poor, and follow Him. The rich man balked — but he went away changed. His encounter with Jesus made him realize he loved his money more than anything else in the world. He couldn't bring himself to let go of his riches, but deep inside he knew he was a pauper for not having done so.

When Jesus whispered to you through the door of your heart: "I love you, my child; your repentant heart is forgiven," your life was forever changed. At that very moment He gave you His Spirit and empowered you to be like Him. In fact, that is what you have been called to do — to follow in His steps (1 Pet. 2:21). By doing so, others see God in you and develop a thirst to know Him personally. Through God at work in your surrendered life, you give others the knowledge that you are different from the rest, and you leave them with an awareness that what you have is missing from their lives.

Have you totally surrendered your life to God? Have you yielded all of yourself to Him and His activity in your life? Have you asked God to change:

the way you talk to your kids?

the way you relate to your spouse?

the way you respond to a manipulative coworker?

the way you deal with the homeless person on the street?

THE MAIN THING

You know you are
being transformed
when you go
beyond asking,
"What would Jesus
do?"and start
asking "What is
Jesus doing in
me?"

CHECK POINT

Memorize the words
of Jesus in John
14:6-7. "I am the
way, and the truth
and the life. No one
comes to the Father
except through me. If
you really knew me,
you would know my
Father as well. From
now on you do know
him and have seen
him."

the way you act when you stand in a long line?
the way you respond to a reckless driver?
the way you spend your money?
the way you spend your time?
the way you live *"your everyday, ordinary life — your
sleeping, eating, going-to-work, and walking around life"*
(Rom. 12:1, THE MESSAGE)?[11]

God's love for you is so great He sent His Son to die for you. That
changed everything. Now, you may be the only glimpse of Jesus some people
will ever have. Will you totally surrender your "walking-around life" to
God's transforming power, so that your life will forever change the lives of
others as Jesus' life did? Will you preface your life choices with the question:
"How will it affect my relationship with Jesus?" Dallas Willard hits the nail
on the head with this statement: "Our inner lives will be transformed when
we ask Jesus to 'take charge of our life' and set out to put into practice everything He said was right."[12]

Who's in charge of *your* life?

This Is Your Life: *Time for a Change*

What areas of your life are you reluctant to ask God to change?

_____
_____
_____
_____

What areas of your life have already been transformed because of God's work?

_____
_____
_____
_____

Day Three: What's Love Got to Do with It?

A popular song asks a question that deserves an answer: *"What's love got to do with it?"* For the Christian, the answer is absolutely everything. Love is the root command of the entire Bible. It is the central characteristic of God. And it must be your central characteristic if you are to love others as Jesus loves you (John 13:34).

Look at Jesus: He sacrificed all, suffered all, and denied all self so that you would see how absolutely amazing, unlimited, and unswerving God's love is (John 3:16). Jesus loved unconditionally with His whole heart. And that's what you are commanded to do (John 15:9).

We're not talking about easy love here. The Bible doesn't focus its primary love directives on the children who give you kisses every day, or on your spouse who stands by you through thick and thin, or on the friend who brings you chicken soup when you're sick. Those people are easy to love. Instead the Bible commands you to love those who spit in your face — and those who break your heart (John 17:18; Matt. 5:44).

And that's hard to do — so hard, in fact, that to love others as Jesus loves them is not something you can do on your own. You need the empowering help of the Holy Spirit. Why? Because you will have to sacrifice to live that kind of love; you will have to bleed a little to live that kind of love; part of you will even have to die to live that kind of love.

Jesus endured the spiteful, hypocritical jabs of the Pharisees — and loved them anyway. Jesus felt the traitorous kiss of Judas — and loved him anyway. Jesus looked at those who drove the nails in His hand and the spear in His side and loved them anyway. Jesus loved in a world heavy with hate. He stood out because of it. And He changed the world with His love. When Jesus loved, hate trembled and crawled back into the abyss from which it came. And God was glorified.

When you love — really love — what happens?

Think back to last week's lesson about the mother of the young college student who died senselessly. Imagine how she must have felt when she looked at her son's body in a casket. Her son, who would never throw his cap into the air at his college graduation; her son, who would never wait at the end of an aisle for his bride; her son, who would never know the joy of being a parent. Never. Never. Never.

"A new command I give you: Love one another. As I have loved you, so you must love one another" (John 13:34).

"For God so loved the world that he gave his only begotten son that whosoever should believe in him should not perish but have everlasting life" (John 3:16, KJV).

"As the Father has loved me, so have I loved you. Now remain in my love" (John 15:9).

"As you sent me into the world, I have sent them into the world" (John 17:18).

"But I tell you: Love your enemies and pray for those who persecute you" (Matt. 5:44).

The anger, hurt, and bitterness must have been overwhelming. But when she asked God to forgive her of her own sins, He began miraculously changing her capacity to love and forgive others.

Could you love someone responsible for your child's death? No, you couldn't. Not on your own. This mother couldn't have loved Jim on her own either. No human can generate love like that. But God can create it in a willing heart (2 Cor. 5:14). And by giving her broken but willing heart to God, this mom became like Jesus. And through his own repentance and God's acceptance of him, so did Jim. Today that transforming and empowering love of God enables both of these ordinary people to love in an extraordinary way. They love in a world heavy with hate. They stand out because of it. And they are changing the world with their love. When these two people love, hate trembles and crawls back into the abyss from which it came. And God is glorified.

You, too, are blessed with that kind of empowering love; it's part of the new spiritual nature you received when God accepted you as His child. But have you fully surrendered to God's desire to show extraordinary love to others through you? Let's see.

Think of two people you don't like (much less love). List their names and the reasons you don't like these individuals:

_____

_____

_____

_____

Now, think of someone who doesn't like you. List that person's name along with the reasons you think that person doesn't like (much less love) you.

_____

_____

_____

_____

If you and the three individuals you listed above were the only people to walk this earth, do you think Jesus would have died just for you and those three other people? The answer is absolutely yes. Why? Because He loves you deeply, in spite of your faults, and He deeply loves those you don't like – in spite of their faults.

Do you have the courage to ask God to empower you with that kind of sacrificial love? Do you have the courage to pray every day that you will come to love those three people as Jesus loves them — despite what they may have done to you? No matter how horrendous?

God's desire is to bring you into a new relationship with Him and with people, especially those who spit in your face and break your heart. And He empowers you through the Holy Spirit to do it (John 13:35; 14:21,23).

Ask God to use your broken, willing heart as a source of love for those who seem unlovable. The seeds of unconditional love are already planted there. Ask Him to help you love as Jesus loved — to help you stop seeing, feeling, and acting with hate and malice the way the world does; but instead to be transformed — to see things the way Jesus saw them, to feel the way Jesus felt, and to act the way He acted. To love the way He loved. To make hate tremble. To let others see Jesus in you and give the glory to God.

This Is Your Life: *Amazing Love*

If your desire is to love the way Jesus loved, pour out your heart to God in written prayer, just as that mother did. Ask God to infuse you with the power of the Holy Spirit to help you love the people you listed as He loves them. Tell God where you are "stuck" with these relationships. Tell him why you are angry with these people. Repent of the chains of hate that shackle your heart and ask God to set you free from them. Ask Him to give you a loving heart like His.

My Prayer

_____

_____

_____

_____

_____

_____

_____

_____

_____

_____

THE MAIN THING

You can't copy the love of Jesus; but God can create it in your willing, broken heart.

CHECK POINT

If you think you've never seen a miracle, think again. You are one!

Day Four: Trust and Obey

Terry Jackson, a chemotherapy nurse in a children's cancer ward, has the job of prying for any tiny vein available in an often emaciated arm. Into these fragile openings he must begin chemical injections that sometimes last as long as 12 hours and are often quite painful. He is probably the greatest pain-giver the children ever meet in their stay in the hospital. But because Terry has battled cancer and its excruciating pain himself, his heart is very open. He treats his responsibilities to the children as a "laying on of hands with love and acceptance." There is little in him that causes him to withdraw. He is a warm, open presence who encourages the children to trust. And it is Terry whom the children most often ask for at the time they are dying. Although he is the main pain-giver; he is also the main love-giver.[13]

Clearly these children put their trust in Terry because he continually demonstrates his love and acceptance of them — and because he himself has endured such pain. Their obedience to his directions is based on their total trust that he knows what is best for them.

Jesus is the main love-giver in your life. He encourages you to trust and obey because He knows what is best for you. In His daily life Jesus demonstrated obedience to God. When He followed God's leading and was baptized by John in the Jordan River, God expressed His immense pleasure with this obedience (Matt. 3:13-17). But the obedience of Jesus did not stop there. Just like the cancer-stricken children, Jesus Himself learned obedience through intense suffering (Heb. 5:8-9). His unwavering obedience, even in death, demonstrated that to love God is to trust Him and to obey His commands — no matter the cost — because of the ultimate glory that results from such sacrifice.

That kind of trust and obedience is what God wants of you. When you look at the sacrificial love of Jesus how can you not totally trust someone who died in your place? Doesn't that prove that He has your best interests at heart? Jesus' total sacrifice for you should dispel any doubt you might have in His ability to guide your life — no matter how gloomy the outlook may seem at the time. Remember, He sees the whole picture, not just a jagged edge; and that should instill confidence in you to totally trust Him, to lay your life at His feet without constantly trying to snatch pieces of it back (John 14:1).

One thing needs to be clear however: Trust isn't the same as the popular view of hope. Committing yourself to trust in Jesus takes you beyond mere hope. *Hope* believes in a positive outcome for a person's life or a particular situation. *Trust* in Jesus rests in the assurance that God is in control — whatever the outcome.

Do you have that kind of unerring trust in Jesus? Are you obeying His commands for your life because of your love and trust of Him? If not, why not? Why are you holding on to pieces of your life when you can't see the big picture but He can? It's God's job to transform your life, not yours. All He asks is that you, like a cancer-stricken child, put your total trust in Him, place your trembling hand in His steady one, and obey His leading (John 14:12,15,21,23). If you lean into God with that depth of trust, He will change the way you think. He will change the way you act. He will change the way you live. He will change the way you love. And the result will be a stronger faith and a life that glorifies God.

This Is Your Life: The Face of Trust

Name someone you totally trust.

_____

Why do you trust this person?

_____
_____
_____
_____

If Jesus is the most trustworthy of all, having proved His love by dying for you, why do you think you sometimes fail to trust Him?

_____
_____
_____
_____

Describe an incident when you didn't trust Jesus for the solution to a problem.

_____
_____
_____
_____

"Do not let your hearts be troubled. Trust in God; trust also in me" (John 14:1).

"I tell you the truth, anyone who has faith in me will do what I have been doing. He will do even greater things than these, because I am going to the Father.... If you love me, you will obey what I command....Whoever has my commands and obeys them, he is the one who loves me. He who loves me will be loved by my Father, and I too will love him and show myself to him.... If anyone loves me, he will obey my teaching. My Father will love him, and we will come to him and make our home with him" (John 14:12, 15,21,23).

God's job is to transform your life; your job is to trust Him and obey Him.

As hard as it may be to do, stop and pray for the individuals from Day Three that you don't like. Ask God to give you the opportunities to show Christlike love to them.

What was the result?

_____
_____
_____
_____
_____

What do you think the result would have been if you had trusted God and obeyed Him in this instance instead of taking things into your own hands?

_____
_____
_____
_____
_____

Describe an incident when you did trust Jesus for the solution to a problem.

_____
_____
_____
_____
_____

What was the result?

_____
_____
_____
_____

What would change in your life if you put your total trust in Him?

_____
_____
_____
_____
_____

Day Five: The Glory Shines Through

Have you ever sat in the quiet stillness of the early dawn and watched the sun rise? At first there are just hints of an orange-red glow, scant promises of the visual drama that is to come. Slowly, fingers of brilliant yellows and golds reach out to touch the sky. Then other hues break through, infusing those first lights with ever greater brilliance. It's a truly glorious unveiling of God's creativity at work. As you stare at His handiwork, you know in your heart there is no greater artist than He (Ps. 19:1).

Just as a sunrise says, *"This is the day the Lord has made"* (Ps. 118:24), your life as a believer is intended to say, "This is a child the Lord has made." As you fully surrender to Him, God works in your life so that Jesus lives His life in you. And as a result, God is glorified by what He does in your life before a watching world (John 17:10). You are His vessel, an instrument of His peace, and your life's purpose is simple: To glorify God with every fiber of your being, with every step you make, and with every breath you take so that the world will come to know Jesus in you.

The life of Jesus was all about glorifying God for the great things He had done. Great things — like sending His Son to die for a world that didn't deserve such a supreme sacrifice. Great things — like proving, once and for all, that hate cannot prevail over the purity of love. Great things — like miraculously changing your self-directed, willful heart into one that loves, trusts, and obeys, a heart that shines like a beacon in a world shuttered in darkness. You may not feel like God shines through you, but the glow that glorifies God is rising in your life as surely as the sun rises. It matters not whether the Spirit makes of you a flaming Paul or a faithful John; what matters is, He is making you like the Lord Jesus, "from glory to glory" (Matt. 5:16).

List some of the ways God shines through you.

_____

_____

_____

_____

If you had difficulty with your list, then know this: God shines through you when you love your spouse more than you love yourself. He shines through you when you follow His will, not your own. He shines through you when you obey His leading, not the world's push. God shines through you when you take another's trembling hand in yours and share the pain. He shines through you when you nurture a child or someone else in need. When you do these things, or an endless list of other everyday acts of love and grace, Jesus is living His life in you. God is glorified. And the shine is brilliantly broadcast to the world.

God's full intention is to call to Himself a people born of the Spirit, people who possess a new nature and a new identity in Jesus, people who live life empowered by love, trust, and obedience, and whose only joy is in glorifying God (2 Cor. 3:18; Phil. 2:15).

In his book *A Long Obedience in the Same Direction,* Eugene Peterson sums up the mission of the Christian life: "The main thing is not to work for the Lord; it is not suffering in the name of the Lord; it is not teaching Sunday School for the Lord; it is not being responsible for the sake of the Lord in the community; it is not keeping the Ten Commandments; nor loving your neighbor; nor observing the golden rule. [As the first article of the Westminster Confession states] the chief end of man is to glorify God and enjoy Him forever."[14] In practical terms this means to be like Jesus in every way — wherever you are. The glory of God flowed like a river from Jesus. And day by day, moment by moment, His glory will flow from your surrendered life, too.

This Is Your Life: God Shines Through You

Use these next moments to lift your personal praise to God who loves you beyond measure. Sing the following chorus as your anthem of love and devotion. Realize that it is through Jesus living out His life in you that God is glorified. If you don't know this tune, make up your own!

> *Shine, Jesus, shine,*
> *Fill the land with the Father's glory;*
> *Blaze, Spirit, blaze,*
> *Set our hearts on fire.*
> *Flow, river, flow,*
> *Flood the nations with grace and mercy;*
> *Send forth Your Word, Lord,*
> *And let there be light.*[15]

A Moment with Jesus

You are never alone. That's the promise of Jesus. When you became a child of God your days of solo struggling ended. Jesus made sure of that. Although His physical time on earth was short, Jesus asked His Heavenly Father to give you a constant companion for your daily walk on this earth. That close companion is the Holy Spirit, also described in Scripture as the Comforter.

"And I will ask the Father, and he will give you another Comforter to be with you forever — the Spirit of truth — but you know him, for he lives with you and will be in you" (John 14:16-17).

The intention of Jesus was to abide with you in spirit, to provide a constant personal source of wisdom and strength for you. The phrase "another Comforter" has special significance for followers of Jesus. In Greek, the word for "another" means "another of like kind" or "same as." Jesus is saying, "I am going to send another just like me." Thus, while Jesus is no longer in human form, He is always with you in spirit. He knew from His own experience, with the day-to-day struggles of life, that you would need His comfort and guidance, so He promises to never leave your side.

"All this I have spoken while still with you. But the Comforter, the Holy Spirit, whom the Father will send in my name, will teach you all things and will remind you of everything I have said to you" (John 14:25-26).

Comforter means "one who stands beside." An older preacher grasped the purpose and position of the Holy Spirit in his life by praying this simple prayer: "Lord prop me up on my leaning side." The Holy Spirit is that sturdy, permanent prop. Scripture makes the permanence and the empowering strength of the Comforter clear in Romans 8:35, 37-39: *"Who shall separate us from the love of Christ? Shall trouble or hardship or persecution or famine or nakedness or danger or sword? ... No, in all these things we are more than conquerors through him who loved us. For I am convinced that neither death nor life, neither angels nor demons, neither the present nor the future, nor any powers, neither height nor depth, nor anything else in creation, will be able to separate us from the love of God that is in Christ Jesus our Lord."*

Jesus, in the person of the Holy Spirit, lives in your heart now and always.

Jesus Is with You

"And in Closing ..."

As you come to the close of this week's study, spend a few minutes reviewing the lessons.

What do you believe is the most important thing God has taught you this week?

_____

_____

_____

_____

What do you believe is the main action God would have you take based upon this week's study?

_____

_____

_____

_____

Spend some time in prayer. Thank God for speaking to you through your study and ask Him to help you put into life practice what you are learning.

Week 3
Strengthening Your Heart

A military officer knocked on a young woman's door and informed her that her husband had been killed in Vietnam. She later poured out her broken heart to her mother. The young woman pleaded with her mother to help her understand any good, any worthy purpose, that could come from her young husband's death. The mother later told her pastor what her own thoughts had been as she wept and held her only child.

"Fourteen years ago a policeman knocked on my door to tell me my husband had died in an automobile accident. Every day since then I asked myself — and God — how there could be any possible purpose for the pain in my heart. Now, 14 years later, holding my daughter and listening to her plead for someone to help her understand her loss — I knew the answer had come."[16]

The mother's heart, shaped by the Holy Spirit during those 14 years, was ready to be the very presence of Jesus for her own heartbroken child. The mother's heart was one that God knew intimately, for He had walked with her through this same valley of death. Because of that she was able to take her daughter's hand and help her walk a difficult road.

Much of the trouble in your life may be simply part of living in an imperfect world. The effect, however — to transform you into the likeness of Jesus — is a work of the Holy Spirit. What may seem nothing more than pointless pain will be an opportunity for the shaping, molding, transforming power of the Holy Spirit.

Last week you learned how important it is to have a balanced life, to place more emphasis on cultivating a growing intimate relationship with Jesus than on outward spiritual activities. You also learned how God empowers you to love, trust, obey, and thus glorify Him. This week you will look at the various tools God uses to bring about progressive spiritual transformation in your life.

God uses both extraordinary circumstances and ordinary events — to transform you into the likeness of Jesus.

WEEK 3 AT A GLANCE

Day 1
The Power of Living Words

Day 2
The Family That Sticks Together

Day 3
Iron Sharpens Iron

Day 4
Exercises That Shape Your Heart

Day 5
The Lessons of Life

Day One: The Power of Living Words

In the movie *My Life,* a young married man named Bob Jones discovers he will die before his son is born. Because he wants his child to know him personally and wants to help guide him through life, Bob records a video library in which he shares his heart and his wisdom. As the movie closes we see a toddler yelling, "Daddy!" as he points to Bob's image and hears his voice on the video. The child clearly recognizes his Daddy. He listens to him and learns from him, just as Bob hoped he would.[17]

God gave you His Word so that you will know His heart and the wisdom He has to share. His words are the firm foundation on which you are to establish your unique relationship with Him (2 Tim. 3:16-17). Without them, you are a pauper; with them you are endowed with an inheritance of rich wisdom for daily life — wisdom that will give you the knowledge and the freedom to live life as Jesus lived it (John 8:31-32).

Henry Ward Beecher pinpoints the guiding wisdom of God's Word this way: "Let the day have a blessed baptism by giving your first waking thoughts to God. The first hour of the morning is the rudder of the day."[18] And in his book, *Soul Nourishment,* George Mueller captures the vital essence of the Living Word: "I meditate on the Scripture, searching as it were into every verse to get a blessing out of it: not for the sake of the public ministry of the Word, not for the sake of preaching on what I had meditated upon, but for the sake of obtaining food for my soul."[19]

A rudder to guide your life. Food for your soul. That's the purpose of the Bible. Do you need guidance on how to sift through that anger you harbor toward your spouse? It's in God's Word (Eph. 4:26). How about that habit of yelling at your kids when you're tired — and even when you're not? It's in there (Eph. 6:4). Need help to respond as Jesus would to someone who has taken advantage of you? You'll find it there (Luke 6:29-31). Need a good hard kick in the pants for being selfish? That's in there too (Jas. 3:14-16) — along with wisdom on every aspect of how to be like Jesus as you walk this earth.

Are you locked into this transformational power source? The Word of God connects you with Jesus — just as if He were sitting next to you. It's His autobiography — a living picture of Him. It shows you how He lived and how He loved — and it's your guide for how God wants Jesus to live and love through you. There is no fiction in this incredible book. Just fact. The Bible is alive (Heb. 4:12). It is the real thing. Pure and simple. The truth. The whole truth. And nothing but the truth. (John 17:17).

How many Bibles are in your home right now? Write that number here. _____ If it became a crime to own a Bible in this country and all those you currently possess were taken from you, how many verses of Scripture could you recite by heart and put down on paper? Write the references for the verses you know by heart.

_____
_____
_____
_____
_____

Did you need additional space? If not, then you have cut yourself off from an amazing power source. Contained in each passage of God's Word is a lesson that can transform your life. That's why you need to study the Bible for all it's worth. Engrave its words in your mind and in your heart so that if the Bible were taken from you tomorrow, you could continue to live its truths because they would be an inseparable part of you, woven into the fabric of your mind, your heart, and your life.

Ask God to use His truths to transform your life so that others will see the Word alive in you and be drawn to it. The song "Where the Silence Breaks" captures the freedom that is found when you truly live the power of God's Word.

> When I seek God in the morning I feel like I am free,
> from all the restless voices calling out to me.
> Surrounded by the silence I surrender to the truth,
> that to live where I can listen is all He calls me to.
>
> I want to hear the voice of God no matter what it takes.
> I want to be weak enough to listen and strong enough to wait.
> It's not enough to know He's speaking,
> I want to hear what He has to say.
> So I am standing in the shadow,
> living where the silence breaks.

"If someone strikes you on one cheek, turn to him the other also. If someone takes your cloak, do not stop him from taking your tunic. Give to everyone who asks you, and if anyone takes what belongs to you, do not demand it back. Do unto others as you would have them do to you" (Luke 6:29-31).

But if you harbor bitter envy and selfish ambition in your heart do not boast about it or deny the truth. Such wisdom does not come down from heaven but is earthly, unspiritual, of the devil. For where you find envy, and selfish ambition, there you find disorder and every evil practice (Jas. 3:14-16).

THE MAIN THING

Knowing the truths of the Bible gives you the freedom to live as Jesus lived.

CHECK POINT

Do you have a closer relationship with Jesus today than you had two weeks ago? If not, why not?

_____

_____

_____

_____

I can hear Him in the pages revealing hidden truths,
 Old verses with new answers for what I am going through.
 Like water to the thirsty His Word is light to me,
 I don't want to miss the moment when He is calling me.

I want to hear the voice of God no matter what it takes.
 I want to be weak enough to listen and strong enough to wait.
 It's not enough to know He's speaking,
 I want to hear what He has to say.
 So I am standing in the shadow,
 living where the silence breaks.[20]

This Is Your Life: Words for the Wise

The great evangelist and theologian John Wesley wrote: "O give me that Book! At any price give me the Book of God! I have it. Here is knowledge enough for me. Let me be [a man of one book]."[21]

How vital it is that you, like Wesley, cherish and thirst for the Word of God. Today it is so easy to have access to God's Word. But what would you do if the blessing of reading the Word of God daily became a blessing of the past? Imagine for a moment that all Bibles in the world will be destroyed one year from today. The only traces of the written Word will be those that you commit to memory. If you memorize one verse per week for a year you'll have 52 verses to guide you through your life. If you memorize one verse a day for a year, you'll have 365 verses to guide you through your life. If you memorize none . . . .

Don't let the Book of Truth that can transform your life collect dust on a table. Immerse yourself in it so that it becomes your rudder. Feed your soul with its wisdom. Start by memorizing 2 Corinthians 3:18 and Romans 12:1-2, which appear on pages 6 and 7 of your study guide.

Write your commitment to study the Bible and memorize its words here. I _____ pledge to honor Christ and my growing relationship with Him by memorizing _____ Scripture verses every _____. I will keep myself accountable by asking _____ to be my Scripture partner.

Day Two: The Family That Sticks Together

BY THE BOOK

Train up a child in the way that he should go and when he is old he will not depart from it (Prov. 22:6).

The old man sat in his rocking chair every afternoon, whittling on a stick. His grandkids would come home from school and peer from the shavings littering their grandpa's feet to what was taking shape in his hands. Although he could create amazing things with a stick and a knife, the old man was more interested in shaping the kids who watched his every move.

The only thing this man knew better than what his grandkids were up to was what the Bible had to say about lying, stealing, laughing at others, and sassing your mom. As they sat at his feet, these eager children learned Bible verses to the tune of that squeaking rocker. Their grandpa always made it fun, giving whatever he shaped from a stick — a spinning top, a little book, or a cross — to the one who got a grip on a verse first, or at least the one who tried the hardest. He often said kids were like sticks — give 'em a little whittle here, a soft touch there, and a good thump on the head occasionally, and they'd become someone you could be proud of.

Years later, those eager grandkids now have children of their own and the old creaky rocker sits still and silent. But the grandchildren of that wise old man can still remember the verses they learned at his feet. They'll carry them in their minds and their hearts forever.

In the jewelry box of a young mother, a small wooden cross holds a place of honor. It was once a rough stick shaped by an old man's hands. Now it's a reminder that her grandfather loved her enough to gently whittle away her roughness to get to something a lot more pleasing to the eye and to God (Prov. 22:6).

Now, when one of her own kids stands on her last nerve, she rubs her fingers over that smooth wooden cross, and she thanks God for a creaky rocking chair, a wise old man, and a stick that was transformed in his gentle hands. Then she reaches out to the children God has entrusted to her — and whittles a little more.[22]

One of the greatest responsibilities a person can have is to be a parent. Why? Because God uses the family unit as a cocoon for spiritual transformation. He wants you to give your children an inheritance of godly wisdom. Deuteronomy 6:6-7 gives parents a clear assignment: *"These commandments that I give you today are to be upon your hearts. Impress them on your children. Talk about them when you sit at home and when you walk along the road, when you lie down and when you get up."*

THE MAIN THING

Family members are one of God's greatest channels of the wisdom that leads to spiritual transformation.

CHECK POINT

Recite a new Scripture verse that you have recently learned. Write it down as a reminder of your commitment to learn God's Word by heart.

_____

_____

_____

_____

_____

_____

Timothy's mother Eunice was a shining New Testament example of a mother who took these words to heart and committed herself to teaching her son God's way. Timothy's life bore witness of her devoted efforts. To have parents who teach you God's ways from His Word is a priceless treasure. To be a parent who loves enough to make the first whittle on a child's life is a high and precious calling. Following this calling not only gives your children and grandchildren early glimpses of God's amazing love and strength, it also provides fresh opportunities for you to learn God's ways even as you seek to guide your child or grandchild.

If you had a "whittler" in your life as a child, thank God for him or her right now. Take the time to stop and recall all the godly truths this loved one shared with you. Then honor that person's Christ-like life by dedicating yourself to shaping the children God puts in your life. One whittle at a time.

This Is Your Life: *Wisdom of the Ages*

Describe a spiritual lesson you learned as a child from a parent or other godly relative.

_____

_____

How do you think you would have learned this truth if this person had not taken the time to gently carve it into your heart?

_____

_____

Ask God to make your heart receptive to a family member who has godly truths to pass on to you. Write that person's name.

_____

If you've resisted attempts by family members to pass on godly wisdom to you, ask yourself why you are resistant and write that reason.

_____

_____

Pray that God will break down your resistance to this source of spiritual transformation and that your own children will not put up walls to such a powerful, yet tender, tool of transformation.

Day Three: Iron Sharpens Iron

Joe Nu'u, a Samoan teenager growing up in the Watts district of Los Angeles, was a 280-pound, 6' 1" gang member— full of anger toward white people for who they were and for what they had. He was quick to admit he had no future and even quicker to use his huge fists to vent his anger and frustration. As a senior in high school Joe was arrested because of his participation in a brutal fight in which a police officer was injured. While Joe was awaiting his trial, the vice-principal of his school advised him to attend a junior college in order to get out of the environment he was in. It was at this college that J.B. Rogers, a local pastor, had started a campus ministry. And he was looking for students just like Joe.

One day J.B. knocked on Joe's door and started telling him about the love of Jesus. The words J.B. spoke were foreign to Joe because the definition of love in Watts was cheap. Real cheap. But J.B. was persistent. He visited Joe regularly. Finally, Joe agreed to attend a Bible study that J.B. was leading.

Being the kind of guy he was, Joe didn't want to be embarrassed by being the only one to show up at the study without a Bible. So he stole one. Everything that J.B. talked about that night and everything that Joe read about from his stolen Bible, was just the opposite of what Joe grew up hearing. As he sat surrounded by white people and discussion about the love of Jesus, Joe felt like he had been transported to a different world.

With Easter break fast approaching, J.B. showed up at Joe's door again and asked him to spend the weekend with him and his wife Johnnie. Joe refused initially, but later changed his mind. As he and several other students were standing in line for the evening meal at J.B.'s, it reminded Joe of standing in the welfare line as a child waiting for free food. One question kept coming to Joe's mind: "Did Jesus love me back then when I was standing in that line?"

That evening Joe went to J.B. and told him that, if Jesus was real, he wanted Him in his life. On March 29, Joe's biological birth date, he bowed down on his knees and said, "Lord, if you are real like J.B. says you are, I want you to take over my life." Joe thought to himself: *If God is real, He'll have to prove it.*

The following day Joe appeared in court to face the possibility of a 15-year prison sentence for his involvement in the fight. To Joe's surprise, his lawyer informed him that all charges against him had been dropped. Joe asked when this decision was made. His attorney said it was handed down the

BY THE BOOK

As iron sharpens iron, so one man sharpens another (Prov. 27:17).

...To prepare God's people for works of service, so that the body of Christ may be built up until we all reach unity in the faith and in the knowledge of the Son of God and become mature, attaining to the whole measure of the fullness of Christ. Then we will no longer be infants, tossed back and forth by the waves, and blown here and there by every wind of teaching and by the cunning and craftiness of men in their deceitful scheming. Instead, speaking the truth in love, we will in all things grow up into him who is the Head, that is, Christ. From him the whole body, joined and held

day before in night court about 11:30 p.m. — the time Joe asked God to take over his life.

Joe immediately moved in with J.B. and Johnnie. For the next four years J.B. discipled Joe, helping to sharpen him as a man of God. Joe went on to serve as a pastor and now he is a staffer with the Fellowship of Christian Athletes. He is reaching out to sharpen others for God's glory, just as J.B. reached out to him.[23]

Every believer in the body of Christ is being transformed by the work of the Holy Spirit and is intended to help other believers grow to be like Jesus (Prov. 27:17). This is not an option for those in the church; it's a biblical mandate (Eph. 4:12-16).

But sometimes in today's culture the church can lose its true focus and operate like a social center rather than as a source of spiritual growth and transformation. What results is an entertainment complex — filled with pretty music, glowing words, and vacant hearts.

But God's church is intended to be a transformational training center, a launching pad to send you as a keenly sharpened tool into the world as an ambassador for Christ. Just as a blacksmith forges sharp tools from rough metal, the church, through the work of the Holy Spirit, is intended to sharpen rough believers for His service, to hone away dull edges that may hinder the cause of Christ, to make believers strong enough to stand the tests of fire that the world metes out. Believers, bonding together to challenge one another to become like Jesus, represent one of God's most amazing transformational tools.

How can you begin to bond with other believers? One way is through group worship experiences. By lifting your personal praises to a glorious God in unison with the praises of others, you experience a spiritual bond of joy that is unequaled. The presence of the Lord abounds where hearts are joined to praise Him. When all present come to Him equally humble, equally in awe, and equally thankful for His amazing love, a spiritual metamorphosis takes place. Social, economic, and cultural differences vanish. Separate souls become as one. Angels rejoice. Lives are forever changed. And God is immensely pleased.

The unity of the spirit created through worship is further reinforced by the person-to-person bonding that develops through church fellowship. The church is intended to be a place where all who walk through its doors know that they have found true friends (Prov. 17:17). These friendships become even stronger through the nurturing bond of discipleship as one who is stronger reaches out to one who is weaker. As one who has known the pain of loss kneels down to lift the burden of another. As the young walk with the old, as those who sing give voice to the songless, as those who have experienced the power of prayer teach others how to pray. All the many gifts of the Spirit, all the many parts of the body, come together as one in the church. That's the way God intended it to be. And that's why the church is such a powerful source of transformation for the believer.

Do not merely fill a pew each Sunday. Ask God to fill your heart, expand your spiritual dimensions, and sharpen you by exposing you to the wealth of wisdom, skills, knowledge, and fellowship that the church and its people possess. Then seek to help others in the body of Christ grow into the likeness of Jesus by sharing your own wisdom. It is through a daily intimate walk with Jesus that the people of the church come to know the heart of God. And it is by seeing Jesus in others that we are compelled to ask God to hone the dull edges in our own lives.

Iron does sharpen iron. How sharp are you?

THE MAIN THING

The church is a launching pad to send you as a keenly sharpened tool into the world as an ambassador for Christ.

This Is Your Life: Gaining an Edge

Name two individuals in the fellowship of believers (the church) who have helped sharpen your faith and prepare you for ministry.

_____

_____

How did being around them help accomplish this?

_____

_____

_____

_____

_____

What other areas of your life has God shown you need sharpening?

_____

_____

_____

CHECK POINT

Encountered any lions lately? Remember, your new vision of eternity will help you sing while lions roar. (See p. 26.)

Ask God to show you individuals in your church who could help you be sharpened in these areas. List their names below and ask God to give you the opportunity to learn from these people. It may be by apprenticing under them in a church ministry or by asking one of them to work with you one-to-one.

_____

_____

_____

_____

Now think of someone God may be preparing you to help.

_____

What steps can you take today to be available to this fellow believer?

_____

_____

_____

_____

What steps can you take today to reach out to someone who doesn't know Christ — just as J.B. Rogers reached out to Joe Nu'u?

_____

_____

_____

_____

_____

Day Four: Exercises That Shape Your Heart

A young mother believed it had been easier for her to "work on her spiritual life" before she became a mom. To her, reading the Bible and praying were the only two activities that "counted" spiritually. She had never been taught to see that caring for two young children might become a kind of school of transformation beyond anything she had ever known. Somehow, for her, having a "quiet time" counted toward spiritual devotion, but caring for two children did not. Other believers had failed to teach her that her children brought her new opportunities for growth that she didn't have when she was single.[24]

Have you opened your eyes to the wealth of spiritual exercises God uses to make you more like Jesus? The list certainly isn't limited to prayer, Bible study, fasting, and worship, although these tools are incredibly powerful and important. The list also includes (but is not limited to) parenthood, the discipline of silence, serving others, evangelism, ministry involvement, musical experiences, caring for the environment, stewardship, solitude, confession, meditation on Scripture, and an endless list of ordinary, as well as extraordinary, opportunities.

But remember, spiritual exercises are not intended to gauge how spiritual you are but to create an avenue that God can use to lead you to His heart (1 Tim. 4:7b-8). It's critical to recognize that even the most iron-willed commitment to a spiritual exercise will not make you more holy. Growth in holiness is a gift from God (John 17:17; 1 Thess. 5:23; Heb. 2:11). Such growth develops from obedience with the appropriate motive of love of God and trust in Him. And through the exercising of spiritual disciplines, God strengthens you to better trust and obey Him in every aspect of your life.

Such discipline comes with a caution, however. In his book *The Life You've Always Wanted*, John Ortberg warns that focusing on spiritual disciplines can lead to a rigid, mechanical kind of "spiritual scorekeeping." Rather than to ask, "What is a spiritually disciplined person?" — it may be more important to discover what a disciplined person is *not*.

"A disciplined person is *not* simply someone who exercises many disciplines," stresses Ortberg. "A disciplined person is *not* a highly systematic, rigidly scheduled, chart-making, gold-star-loving early riser. The Pharisees were rigid and organized, but they were not disciplined persons in the sense

BY THE BOOK

Exercise yourself toward godliness. For bodily exercise profits a little, but godliness is profitable for all things, having promise of the life that now is and of that which is to come (1 Tim. 4:7b-8, NKJV).

"Now they know that everything you have given me comes from you" (John 17:7).

May God himself, the God of peace, sanctify you through and through. May your whole spirit, soul, and body be kept blameless at the coming of our Lord Jesus Christ (1 Thess. 5:23).

Both the one who makes men holy and those who are made holy are of the same family. So Jesus is not ashamed to call them brothers (Heb. 2:11).

required by true believers who follow Jesus.

"Spiritual exercises ... are not a barometer of spirituality," emphasizes Ortberg. "The true question you must continually ask yourself then is this: 'Am I growing in love for God and people through this exercise?' The real issue is not what spiritual exercises you are doing but what kind of person you are becoming."[25]

Near the end of his life, Paul took an inventory of sorts to see what type of man he had become (2 Tim. 4:6-8). As he reviewed his journey, Paul saw the offering he had made of his life to the God he loved with his whole heart. Like an athlete who had engaged successfully in a contest, Paul had "fought the good fight" (kept his focus on God's mission for him); he had "finished the race" (gone the distance even when the going was tough); and he had "kept the faith" (carefully lived his life according to the teachings of the Christian faith).

Is your life an offering to God? It can be. Just like Paul, you are an athlete engaged in a contest against the powers of darkness. But you are guided by the light of Jesus. Ask Him to use everyday spiritual exercises, as well as extraordinary ones, to shape your heart. Spiritual exercises are means by which God transforms you and He is glorified. Seek to be transformed through them so that, like Paul, you too can say: "I have fought the good fight, I have finished the race. I have kept the faith."

This Is Your Life: Spiritual Fitness

List some spiritual exercises God is currently using to shape your life.

_____

_____

_____

Describe how God is using these exercises to make you more like Jesus.

_____

_____

_____

_____

What new opportunity for growth do you have today that you didn't have five years ago?

What is stopping you from *growing spiritually fit* from this opportunity?

What new opportunity for growth do you have today that you didn't have two years ago?

What is stopping you from *growing spiritually fit* from this opportunity?

What new opportunity for growth do you have today that you didn't have last month?

What is stopping you from *growing spiritually fit* from this opportunity?

What new spiritual exercise is God opening for you so that He can transform your life in a creative new way?

Exercising Out of the Box

Below is a list of "out-of-the-box" disciplines for spiritual growth:

- Put your television in the attic for six months.
- Give the gift of laughter to someone every day.
- Pick up one piece of trash off the street each day.
- Pledge not to buy an article of clothing for yourself for six months.
- Encourage others by saying the positive, not the negative.
- Remaining silent when others are talking.
- Find opportunities to say "yes" to your kids.
- Say "Good morning, Lord" when you wake up.
- Say prayers with your children every night.

THE MAIN THING

Spiritual exercises are not the barometer of spirituality; they are the means by which you place your life as an offering before God so that He can create holiness in you.

CHECK POINT

Remember, God has given you everything you need to live a life that glorifies Him. How is your life a testimony for the transforming power of your new spiritual DNA?

Day Five: The Lessons of Life

BY THE BOOK

In this you greatly rejoice, though now, for a little while, you may have had to suffer grief in all kinds of trials. These have come so that your faith — of greater worth than gold, which perishes even though refined by fire — may be proved genuine and may result in praise, glory, and honor when Jesus Christ is revealed (1 Pet. 1:6-7).

Our fathers disciplined us for a little while as they thought best; but God disciplines us for our good, that we may share in his holiness. No discipline seems pleasant at the time, but painful. Later on, however, it produces a harvest of righteousness and peace for those who have been trained by it (Heb. 12:10-11).

Luke rested his BB gun on his shoulder and headed for the house. As he walked, he kicked a small bush, startling a stray cat who promptly scratched vigorously at Luke's leg. In attempting to defend himself from this unexpected assault, Luke dropped his BB gun, then promptly tripped over it as he tried to elude the cat's spiteful claws.

Luke's father witnessed this spectacle from the back porch, barely able to contain his laughter. But contain it he did because he held Lacy, who — thanks to her big brother — was having a bad day, too. Clutched in her hand was her favorite doll, the once-perfect face pimpled with BB holes. The doll shed no tears, but Lacy was wailing. As Luke limped toward his father and sister, he was holding back his own tears. But when he saw Lacy, the BB-scarred doll, and the look on his father's face, he knew things were about to get even more painful.

His father passed Lacy into her mother's arms and pointed Luke into the house toward the bathroom. There he gently applied antiseptic to Luke's scratches; then he reached up and thumped Luke on the head with his thumb and forefinger.

Luke winched. "Dad, how can you fix my cuts and thump me on the head all at the same time?"

"I can do both, Luke, because I love you. Now listen up and listen up good. You couldn't avoid that cat; you had no idea she was in that bush, and you got the worst of her temper. It's my job to bandage your wounds and help you learn from unavoidable experiences like that. But that head thump is for using your sister's doll for target practice. It's my job to help Lacy through that hurt and teach her that sometimes people do mean things for no good reason. It's also my job to punish you so you'll think twice next time."

"So the head thump is my punishment?" Luke asked hopefully.

"Nice try, son. But that head thump was only to get your attention. It stings for a little while; your discipline will make a more lasting impression." He finished applying the band aids, then picked up the BB gun that had been resting in the corner of the bathroom. "This is going in the lock box for three months — maybe more. The next time you have it in your hands, I hope you'll choose a more appropriate target. Now, go get your birthday money. You're going to buy a doll today."

Luke winced. He wouldn't be entering the BB gun bulls-eye contest with his friends tomorrow — or buying that new video game anytime soon. But he knew in his heart that his dad was right. As he walked down the hall, rubbing the sting the thump had made on his head, Luke said, "Dad, I'm sorry. Guess I need to tell Lacy I'm sorry too, huh?"

"That would be a real good idea. And while you are doing that, I'd really like to hear how you thought you were going to get away with filling your sister's doll full of holes...." he added with a grin.[26]

Like it or not, life is filled with an abundance of unavoidable circumstances that cause you pain — and, most likely, an array of avoidable bad choices that necessitate discipline. God uses both circumstances and discipline to transform you into His Son's likeness because of His unconditional love for you (1 Pet. 1:6-7; Heb. 12:10-11). Often tough circumstances are brought about simply by living in a world that isn't perfect.

Think back on an instance when you were the victim of an unavoidable circumstance. Describe that instance and how it made you feel.

_____
_____
_____

At the time you probably wished the situation would just go away. But more than likely the sting of that event stayed around. How did you handle the situation?

_____
_____
_____

What do you think God wanted you to glean from experiencing that type of unavoidable circumstance?

_____
_____
_____

If you encountered a similar situation today, how would you handle it differently and why do you think you would be able to do so?

_____
_____
_____

And we know that in all things God works for the good of those who love him, who have been called according to his purpose.... If God is for us, who can be against us? He who did not spare his own Son, but gave him up for us all — how will he not also, along with him, graciously give us all things? .... No, in all things we are more than conquerors through him who loved us. For I am convinced that neither death nor life, neither angels nor demons, neither the present nor the future, nor any powers, neither height nor depth, nor anything else in all creation, will be able to separate us from the love of God that is in Christ Jesus our Lord (Rom. 8:28, 31b-32,37-39).

Think back to Day Two of this week (p. 53). What godly wisdom have you recently learned from a family member or another person God has put in your life ? Summarize that wisdom here.

_____

_____

_____

_____

_____

_____

_____

_____

Like a good father, God uses circumstances — the ebb and flow of life itself — as a teaching tool, a source of transformation. Such experiences forever change you and make you more capable of living like Jesus. As a result, you are better able to help others who may experience similar circumstances. Like the mother who held her heartbroken daughter in her arms after the death of her husband, comforting her because she herself had known that pain, you too can walk familiar paths with another person. True spiritual transformation isn't without pain and struggle. Jesus' life and death exemplify that. But by trusting and obeying God in the midst of struggles, those trying circumstances can become a garden for heart-changing miracles (Rom. 8:28,31b-32,37-39).

Of course, there is unavoidable circumstance — and then there's the grief you pile on your own head. While it's impossible to live life without getting caught in unpleasant circumstances, you do have much greater control over poor choices that result in God's discipline. Though sad but true, many of life's greatest lessons are learned through making bad choices. It's during those times that God uses loving discipline to prune and shape you. Like young Luke, you may lose things you cherish in the process, but what you lose pales in comparison to gaining the wisdom and heart of Jesus.

And remember this, just as a parent garners no pleasure in disciplining a child, God is not gleefully waiting for you to shoot yourself in the foot so He can zap you. But when He does discipline you and point you in the right direction, rest in the fact that only someone who really loves you and wants the best for you would take the time to do that. God's discipline may not be fun, but it can help turn your hard heart into one like His.

This Is Your Life: The Face of Discipline

Describe an instance in your life when you encountered God's loving discipline.

_____

_____

_____

How did God use that situation to make you more like Jesus?

_____

_____

_____

A Moment with Jesus

Jesus was in great anguish. What lay ahead of Him seemed too much to bear: great physical pain, the weight of the sins of the entire world on His shoulders, and — worst of all — total separation from His Heavenly Father for the first time. This last must have left Him trembling in fear. As He stood in the darkness of the Garden of Gethsemane, Jesus appealed to Peter, James, and John to pray fervently. He made it clear that He was *"overwhelmed with sorrow to the point of death."* But these men who had walked miles with Jesus in the past did not go the distance this time. Instead, they slept. Luke tells us that Jesus *"withdrew about a stone's throw beyond them"* (Luke 22:41a) where *"he knelt down and prayed, 'Father, if your are willing, take this cup from me; yet not my will, but yours be done'"* (Matt. 22:41b-42).

There will be times in your life when the burden gets so heavy you must go a "stone's throw" further than you've ever gone before. What happens when you're willing to go this deep with God?

1. **You will always go alone into God's presence.**

2. **It is in the deeper place where you'll learn that your burdens are lifted with prayer.** The writer of Hebrews says, *"During the days of Jesus' life on earth, he offered up prayers and petitions with loud cries and tears to the one who could save him from death, and he was heard because of his reverent submission"* (Heb. 5:7). Luke says of Jesus *"And being in anguish, he prayed more earnestly, and his sweat was like drops of blood falling to the ground"* (Luke 22:44). This is serious, soul-searching prayer.

3. **It is by going a little further that you'll find the will of God.** When Jesus used the salutation *"Abba, Father,"* He was making the most intimate, the most heart-wrenching appeal of all. And God gave Jesus the most intimate of answers: His death was the only path to life.

4. **When you go a little deeper, you'll find heaven's help.** With all doubt gone, Jesus was empowered for what lay ahead. *"An angel from heaven appeared to Him and strengthened Him"* (Luke 22:43).

5. **When you have gone a little deeper, you'll be ready.** *"Rise let us go!"* Jesus said to His sleeping disciples. *"Here comes my betrayer!"* (Matt. 26:46). Because He was strengthened and assured of God's will for Him, Jesus was ready for arrest, trial, mockery, and death. The disciples were not ready; they had slept through the preparation time. Are you spending intense time in prayer so that you, too, will be ready to do God's will? Or are you sleeping?

Jesus Was Ready

"And in Closing ..."

As you come to the close of this week's study, spend a few minutes reviewing the lessons.

What do you believe is the most important thing God has taught you this week?

_____

_____

_____

_____

What do you believe is the main action God would have you take based upon this week's study?

_____

_____

_____

_____

Spend some time in prayer. Thank God for speaking to you through your study and ask Him to help you put into life practice what you are learning.

Week 4
Your Visible Heart

The story is told of David, whose home was directly across from a cancer clinic. He and his family lived downstairs and rented the upstairs rooms to outpatients at the clinic. One day a stooped and shriveled old man, no taller than a young child, knocked on the door. Half of his face was red, swollen, and oozing a pale liquid.

The old man's voice, however, was pleasant as he said, "Good evening, my name is Seth. I've come to see if you've a room for just one night. I came for treatment this morning from the eastern shore, and there's no bus till morning." Seth explained that he had been looking for a room since noon, but with no success. "I guess it's my face. I know it looks terrible, but my doctor says with a few more treatments...." For a moment David hesitated, but the old man's next words melted his heart: "I could sleep in this rocking chair on the porch. My bus leaves early in the morning."

Although the rooms upstairs were already full, David told Seth he would find him a bed. As they talked together on the porch that evening, it didn't take David long to see that the ugly old man had a huge beautiful heart squeezed into his tiny, shriveled body. Seth explained that he fished to support his daughter, her five children, and her husband, who was hopelessly crippled. He didn't tell it by way of complaint; in fact, every other sentence was prefaced with a thanks to God for a blessing. Seth was grateful that no pain accompanied his disease, which was a form of skin cancer, and he thanked God for giving him the strength to keep going. At bedtime, David made a cot for Seth in the children's room, who didn't seem at all bothered by the old man's face.

When Seth left that next morning David told him he was welcome in their home whenever he had treatments. The next time Seth came he brought a quart of the largest oysters David had ever seen. Seth said he had shucked them that morning so they'd be nice and fresh. David knew Seth's bus left at 4:30 a.m., and he wondered what time the old man had to get up in order to do that for them. In the year Seth came to stay overnight with David's family, there was never a time when he didn't bring fresh vegetables from his garden. Other times they received packages in the mail by special delivery: fresh fish packed in a box of kale. Knowing that the old man must

The measure of discipleship is the degree to which a believer is like Jesus.

WEEK 4 AT A GLANCE

Day 1
A Shining Example

Day 2
Walk the Words

Day 3
Many Voices, One Calling

Day 4
A World of Difference

Day 5
Get "Real" Different

walk miles to mail these, and knowing how little money he had, made the gifts doubly precious. When David received these remembrances, he often thought of a comment his neighbor made after Seth left that first morning.

"You kept that awful little man last night! I turned him away. You can lose roomers by putting up such people!"

Maybe David did lose roomers once or twice. But if only those patients could have known Seth, perhaps their illnesses would have been easier to bear. David's family will always be grateful to have known Seth; from him they learned what it is to accept the bad without complaint and the good with gratitude to God.

Recently David was visiting a friend who has a greenhouse. As she showed him her flowers, they came to the most beautiful one of them all, a golden chrysanthemum, bursting with bloom. To David's great surprise, it was growing in an old, dented, rusty bucket! David thought, "If this were my plant, I'd put it in the loveliest container I had."

His friend changed his mind.

"I ran short of pots," she explained," and knowing how beautiful this one would be, I thought it wouldn't mind starting out in this old pail. It's just for a little while, till I can put it out in the garden.

She must have wondered why David laughed so delightedly, but he was imagining just such a scene in heaven.

"Here's an especially beautiful one," God might have said when he came to the soul of Seth. "He won't mind starting out in this shriveled body."

And now, in God's garden, how tall this lovely old soul must stand.[27]

Last week you studied the tools God uses to transform your heart. This week you'll look at the things that reveal a transformed heart so that you can recognize the beauty of Seth — whose heart mirrored God's heart — in your own life. For it is through ugly little men and people like you that *"God has chosen to make known among the Gentiles the glorious riches of this mystery, which is Christ in you, the hope of glory"* (Col. 1:27).

The measure of discipleship is the degree to which a believer is like Jesus. May you recognize yourself on the following pages.

Day One: A Shining Example

Irene Webster Smith came from a poor English family and had to work as a housekeeper from a very young age. One day she heard the gospel and asked Jesus to receive her as one of His children. From that moment on, Irene loved to hear the missionaries talk about God's work in far away places. She prayed that God would make it possible for her to one day serve as a missionary. However, although she applied to many mission organizations, Irene was not accepted by any mission board due to her lack of education. But one day a mission group working in Japan advertised for a housekeeper to keep house for a single missionary. With good character and work references Irene was appointed as the housekeeper. She worked hard at the job of scrubbing floors, dishes, and toilets — and just as hard at learning the difficult Japanese language.

Irene soon learned that unwanted Japanese baby girls were often killed or sold to brothels to spend their lives in bondage. There came a time when she felt the call of God to bring into the house she kept so spotless, a little Japanese girl who was unwanted by her parents. Before long, Irene was buying other Japanese girls who were to be sold to brothels. The mission frowned on this ministry and finally released Irene from their support. But Irene was undaunted — and she knew in her heart that she was not alone. Although her hands were rough and red from her daily work, her heart was a thing of beauty. She was a woman of prayer and faith under the total lordship of Christ. Because of Irene's tender obedience, God provided her the money for orphanages, churches, and schools in Japan. She became one of the most famous Christian missionaries in the history of Japan and the only missionary who was trusted to teach the royal family. The Japanese people named her Sensei, which means "honored teacher."

Sensei was the last missionary to leave Japan during World War II and the first to be given a passport to return after the war at the request of General MacArthur, the Military Occupation Commander. She was a willing servant wherever God placed her. Whether she held a scrub brush or the hand of a small child, Sensei was a vessel for the glory of God. And because of her obedience, lives were forever changed.[28]

To shine with love, trust, and obedience — whether you're sharing your testimony or scrubbing a floor — is evidence of a heart resting in the arms of God (2 Tim. 2:21; John 14:21; 2 Cor. 4:6). Perhaps your life isn't turning out the way you dreamed it would; perhaps you're nowhere near where you

By the Book

If a man cleanses himself from the [ignoble], he will be an instrument for noble purposes, made holy, useful to the Master and prepared to do any good work (2 Tim. 2:21).

"Whoever has my commands and obeys them, he is the one who loves me. He who loves me will be loved by my Father, and I too will love him and show myself to him" (John 14:21).

For God, who said, "Let light shine out of darkness" made his light shine in our hearts to give us the light of knowledge of the glory of God in the face of Christ (2 Cor. 4:6).

thought you would be by now. No matter your circumstance, know this: God can shine through you, wherever you are, whatever you're doing. If your heart is fully surrendered to Him, then during every hour of each day God is pleased and glorified by your life. Granted, you may be far from being what He intends to make of you in the future, but He is perfectly pleased with where you are as long as you love Him, trust Him, and obey His leading.

Think of it this way: A little baby is perfectly pleasing to its mother as an infant, yet is far from being what the mother wishes him to be when the years of maturity come. Give yourself some time to grow, but ask God to shine through you wherever you are. As a creative work of God "in progress," live the pure principle of trusting in the God who first created you in your mother's womb and then re-created you in the image of His perfect Son. You may not always understand God's methods, but if you rest by faith in His divine purpose, you'll bring glory to His name and warmth to His heart. And that glory will draw others to Him.

In the big transformational scheme of things, your part is to do the trusting; God's part is to accomplish the results. And when you do your part, He never fails to do His. God never shortchanges any of His children, so don't be discouraged by your status in life. Trust God each day. The matter will not end there. Trust is the beginning and the continual foundation. When you trust, the Lord works; and His work is the important part of the whole matter.

The repulsive face of the fisherman could not hide the fact that his heart was bigger and far more beautiful than his shriveled body. The radiant heart of Sensei could not be clouded by the dust she swept. Your transformed heart cannot be covered by the mud that tracks through your life. The glory of God can never be hidden when love, trust, and obedience are present.

This Is Your Life: *Beyond the Jagged Edge*

Take a look at your life. Have you failed to continually trust God because life hasn't turned out the way you planned? Remember, you can only see the jagged edge of the tapestry that is your life. God has the whole picture in mind. If you have failed to love, trust, and obey Him with all your heart, ask for His forgiveness now.

As an exercise of trust and faith, describe below what you've always dreamed of doing. Then describe where you are in your life today. Stop and thank God for where you are. Then list ways that God can use you as a vessel for His glory right now.

My dream —

_____
_____
_____
_____
_____

Where I am today —

_____
_____
_____
_____
_____
_____

Ways God can use me now —

_____
_____
_____
_____
_____

CHECK POINT

What new spiritual opportunities have you incorporated into your life this month?

_____
_____
_____
_____
_____
_____

How has God used them to change you?

_____
_____
_____
_____
_____
_____
_____
_____
_____
_____

Day Two: Walk the Words

"When Mack Jenkins got religion, he came here and told me he had religion, and he wanted to kneel down and kiss my foot because I had been a slave and he wanted to humble himself to me. I said, 'Jenkins, if you don't get away from here, I'm gonna haul back and kick you in the mouth. Religion raises the heart, makes you noble, it don't make you crazy,' I said. 'If I was you I would check again to see what I really got.' "[29]

What have *you* "really got?" In this fictional autobiography, Miss Jane Pitman hit the nail on the head when she explained, in her own unique way, that Mack Jenkins needed to lose his religion and get relationship. Because spiritual transformation isn't about grand demonstrations. The teachings of Jesus permeate every aspect of your life. It's walking His words, day in and day out, not just talking them. Religion might, in fact, have you kissing feet and acting crazy. But relationship is no act. Its intimacy takes your heart of stone and transforms it into a heart of grace. As a truly transformed believer you live what you have internalized, you love God and others the way Jesus loved them, and you bear fruit because of Whose you are — not because of who's watching (John 15:8).

In Matthew 11:28-30 Jesus says, *"Come to me ... learn from me ... and you will find rest for your souls."* Do you come to Jesus with every decision, every question, every relationship in your life so that you can be guided by the wisdom that is found in the Scriptures? So that you can rest in the knowledge that the decisions you make are pleasing to God? The question "How will this affect my relationship with Jesus?" is the lens through which you should look at every aspect of your life. This focus should drive you to the Scriptures to discover biblical answers to life's questions. Such a biblically guided life will impact all your relationships — husband-wife, parent-child, friends, coworkers, and church family, as well as the lost, and society in general. It will create in you the fruit of the spirit — love, joy, peace, patience, kindness, goodness, faithfulness, gentleness, and self-control, which will, in turn, produce more fruit. For when God's Word permeates your actions, "good fruit" is produced wherever you are, whomever you're with, whatever you're doing (Matt. 12:33).

Think of the last two major decisions you have made in your life. Write those decisions.

_____

_____

Describe how each of those decisions affected your relationship with Jesus. Did they make it stronger? Weaker?

_____

_____

_____

What process did you use to make those decisions?

_____

_____

_____

Would asking the question "How will this affect my relationship with Jesus?" have changed the decisions you made? If so, how?

_____

_____

_____

Discipleship at its foundation is a change of heart that expresses itself in the outward life. Commit today to using the lens of Scripture as the filter for your life and the world around you. No aspect of your life is segregated from your spiritual life — or at least it shouldn't be. Jesus has given you a guidebook to teach you how to live. Absorb it and live it out loud. It is the essence of who you are in Christ — and the evidence to others that you, too, know the wise and wonderful Jesus by heart.

This Is Your Life: Question of the Day

As you go through today, filter each decision you must make (whether it's to take a shortcut on a project, to zip through a yellow light, to give money to a homeless person, or to volunteer for a project at church) through this question: "How will this decision affect my relationship with Jesus?" You may find yourself making different decisions today than you did yesterday.

THE MAIN THING

Spiritual transformation isn't about grand demonstration. The teachings of Jesus permeate every aspect of your life.

CHECK POINT

List three ways God has shined through you this week.

_____

_____

_____

_____

_____

_____

Day Three: Many Voices, One Calling

BY THE BOOK

"I will remain in the world no longer, but they are still in the world, and I am coming to you. Holy Father, protect them by the power of your name — the name you gave me — so that they will be one as we are one" (John 17:11).

I, therefore, the prisoner of the Lord, beseech you to walk worthy of the calling with which you were called, with all lowliness and gentleness, with longsuffering, bearing with one another in love, endeavoring to keep the unity of the Spirit in the bond of peace. There is one body and one spirit, just as you were called in one hope of your calling: one Lord, one faith, one baptism, one God and Father of all, who is above all, and through all, and in you all (Eph. 4:1-5, NKJV).

Beth takes the east hall to the meeting room; she doesn't want to walk by Nancy's office because she *"gets on my nerves with that holier-than-thou attitude."* Ben withheld key research information from Derrick because he refused to vote the way Ben wanted him to in the last planning meeting. Derrick won't help Ben make an important deadline because he has a different opinion about the way the project should be handled. John is irritated with Leslie because she went home before accomplishing everything he put on her "to-do" list....

Sound like the typical cut-throat, watch-your-back corporation? It could be your local church. Sadly, the body of Christ is sometimes a cauldron of bickering, backstabbing, manipulation, competition, selfishness, and dissension. That's not what God wants. And it's certainly not what the world needs. What the world needs and what God wants is unity in the body of Christ, which has been modeled by the Father and the Son — the kind of unity that demonstrates a bonding of the spirit, a joint focus on the same goal (John 17:11).

A heart like His is a garden for such unity. It denies self and works toward unity as a powerful witness to the reality of God's selfless love — in spite of a melting pot of personalities, opinions, gifts, and perspectives. It possesses an understanding that there are many different voices in the body of Christ but one calling. And that calling is to glorify God (Eph. 4:1-5).

How can you recognize if yours is a selfless heart focused on its calling? Such a heart cultivates unity in the body of Christ by praying for other Christians, by avoiding gossip, by building others up, by working together in humility, by exalting Christ, and by refusing to get sidetracked arguing over details. It's a peaceful heart, not a warring one. Does that sound like you?

Briefly summarize a recent difference of opinion you have had with another Christian.

_____

_____

_____

_____

_____

What was the real root cause of this disagreement?

_____

_____

Do you think God was glorified by the way you approached this situation?

_____

_____

If maintaining unity in the spirit (and thus glorifying God) had been your focus rather than accomplishing your short-term goal, do you think you would have acted differently and achieved different results? If so, how?

_____

_____

_____

Do you need to go to this person and restore unity in your relationship? If so, write that person's name as a pledge to heal this break in the body of Christ this week.

_____

Jesus demonstrated humility and self-denial in His relationship and sacrifice for the church. That did not mean He became a wimpy push-over. Far from it. But His conduct was always based on His calling — to glorify God. His ability to love and self-sacrifice for others was empowered by His constant unity with God. Likewise, your unity with others in the body of Christ is empowered by the Holy Spirit, who brings believers together into a dedicated and distinct relationship with the Father, united as one spiritual family. If you are living in unity with God, you'll live in unity with others. It's only when you allow your self-interest to reign in your life that unity with others becomes severed (Rom. 15:5-7).

Bickering, finger pointing, back stabbing, nail biting, mud slinging, and hand wringing don't glorify God. (But they do make Satan dance a gleeful jig.) Look around you. Are you a unifying force or a divisive one? Is God being glorified by your actions or are you providing a soundtrack for Satan's dance?

The love of Jesus overcomes envy, jealousy, frustration, and selfishness — the core of much dissension in the body of Christ (Phil. 2:1-6). And this love directs the church to its primary goal — to glorify God. The visible, trans-

May the God who gives endurance and encouragement give you a spirit of unity among yourselves as you follow Christ Jesus, so that with one heart and mouth you may glorify the God and Father of our Lord Jesus Christ. Accept one another, then, just as Christ accepted you, in order to bring praise to God (Rom. 15:5-7).

If you have any encouragement from being united with Christ, if any comfort from his love, if any fellowship with the Spirit, if any tenderness and compassion, then make my joy complete by being like-minded, having the same love, being one in spirit and purpose. do nothing out of selfish ambition or vain conceit, but in humility consider others better than yourselves. Each of you should look not only to your own interests, but also to the interests of others. Your attitude should be the same as that of Jesus Christ (Phil. 2:1-6).

THE MAIN THING

The body of Christ is filled with many different voices, but we are called to sing the same song: Glory to His name.

CHECK POINT

Recite 2 Corinthians 3:18. This Scripture appears on page 6 of this book.

formed heart hears this calling and reaches out to join hands with other believers — believers of different perspectives, different gifts, different races, different working styles — so that all can join together to sing in unison:

> *Make us one, Lord, make us one.*
> *Holy Spirit, make us one.*
> *Let your love show so the world will know*
> *We are one with You.*[30]

To know Jesus by heart is to accept His lordship in all areas of your life and to share His values, His perspective, and His commitment to love other Christians. Granted, sometimes it's not easy. It may take years of prayer to build unity with some people. But God can create unity even where you think it's impossible. And when it is done, you'll be amazed to find that the person who has changed the most is you.

There are many voices in the body of Christ, but only one true calling. May you grow to love the unique melody made by each as you glorify God together.

This Is Your Life: "God, There's a Fly in My Soup."

Who's the spot on your tie? The snag in your stockings? The fly in your soup? The one fellow believer who makes you grit your teeth? Write that person's name.

_____

Will you commit to pray for this person every day for the next two weeks? Don't ask God to change this person. Ask God to change your heart toward this person so that He can create unity between your two hearts. By doing so you honor the calling of Christ — and you just might be surprised at what God will do with the two of you. If you pledge before God to pray for "the fly in your soup" every day for the next two weeks, sign your name.

_____

Day Four: A World of Difference

Madonna. Mother Teresa. Two women with totally different approaches to life. Material Girl Madonna has made millions pursuing self-satisfaction. The world deems her a success because of the millions she has amassed — and perhaps because of the millions of people she has made gasp by her provocative behavior. Mother Teresa rarely had two nickels to rub together during her lifetime, and if she did she gave them to the poor. But with a heart like His she dedicated herself to pouring out God's love to everyone she met. Doing so wasn't her life's work; it was the light of her life. Loving others as Jesus loved them, serving wherever she went, was God's calling for her. And she was happy fulfilling it. Her inner joy bubbled to the surface of her life and overflowed onto everyone she touched. Even a material world blinded by selfish greed recognized the richness of her spirit.

In the years to come Madonna may be remembered for making a statement. But Mother Teresa will be remembered for making a difference.

As a transformed believer you, too, are called to make a difference in this world (John 17:4-5). God has called you to see the world as Jesus did — to love the lost so much that God speaks His message of redemptive love through you. He has called you to be a contagious Christian, one who spreads the love of God to every person you meet. He is calling you to live your life so that those you touch for Him will, in turn, touch others who will touch still more. Through such contagious Christianity, the love of God spreads like a vigorous kudzu vine, growing by leaps and bounds every day.

But while you're loving the lost of the world, you must not lose yourself in the world's mire. Realize, as Jesus did, that your heart, soul, mind, and attitude are possessed by God and must be kept apart from the world's enticements. Otherwise, the mud in which you serve will become the mud in which you slip and fall (John 17:15-18).

How do you keep your footing sure? Your mind and heart must be continually strengthened through a daily growing relationship with Jesus Christ, a continual learning process that ensures a firm foundation — even when the muck and mire of the world are swirling around you (Rom. 12:1-2). Your personal relationship with Christ guides you to the Scriptures, which present a strong biblical worldview — a steady and sure plumb line that should guide how you think and act (2 Tim. 3:16-17).

As you come to know Jesus by heart, you'll lose your taste for the plastic things the world offers up; you'll be satisfied only by the richness of God (Col.

By the Book

"I have brought you glory on earth by completing the work you gave me to do. As you sent me into the world, I have sent them into the world" (John 17:4-5).

"My prayer is not that you take them out of the world but that you protect them from the evil one. They are not of the world, even as I am not of it. Sanctify them by the truth; your word is truth. As You sent me into the world, I have sent them into the world" (John 17:15-18).

Therefore, I urge you, brothers, in view of God's mercy, to offer your bodies as living sacrifices, holy and pleasing to God — this is your spiritual act of worship. Do not conform any longer to the pattern of this world, but be transformed by the renewing of your mind. Then you will

3:2). In fact, you'll crave the richness of God. And this transformation will make a world of difference in the way you live in a secular society and the way you seize God-given opportunities to make a difference in the world. You won't be fearful about spreading the gospel; you'll be fervent about it. You won't be casual about your faith; you'll become committed to it. You won't be satisfied with making an appearance; you'll be determined to make a difference.

No doubt about it — Madonna is different. But Jesus made a difference. And because of Jesus, Paul made a difference. Mother Teresa made a difference. The coliseum Christians made a difference.

Are you making a difference?

This Is Your Life: Different Strokes

Think of two people you know who are not believers. Write their names.

_____

_____

List ways God can touch them through you this week with His love.

_____

_____

_____

_____

_____

_____

_____

_____

A wise person once said, "You may not be what you think you are, but you are what you think." This quote summarizes the reality of a life that makes a difference in this world. Its premise is based on the truths of Philippians 4:8-9: *"Finally, brothers, whatever is true, whatever is noble, whatever is right, whatever is pure, whatever is lovely, whatever is admirable — if anything is excellent or praiseworthy — think about such things. Whatever you have learned or received or heard from me, or seen in me — put it into practice. And the God of peace will be with you."*

Think of what the apostle Paul was like before his conversion. Then think of what God was able to accomplish for His glory through Paul. Now think about what God can accomplish through you.

How can God use you to change the world?

_____
_____
_____
_____
_____
_____

Ask God to give you daily insight to discern godly ways to evoke positive change in the world around you.

THE MAIN THING

You can make a difference by loving the people in this world but not by loving the things of this world.

CHECK POINT

What have you learned recently from an unavoidable circumstance in your life? (See pp. 62-64.)

_____
_____
_____
_____

How about your poor choices that have produced discipline? What have you learned from those lately? (See pp. 62-64.)

_____
_____
_____
_____

Day Five: Get "Real" Different

BY THE BOOK

For it is by grace you have been saved through faith — and this is not from yourselves, it is the gift of God — not by works so no one can boast (Eph. 2:8-9).

"But the seed on good soil stands for those with a noble and good heart, who hear the word, retain it, and by perseverance produce a good crop" (Luke 8:15).

For everyone born of God overcomes the world. This is the victory that has overcome the world, even our faith. Who is he that overcomes the world? Only he who believes that Jesus is the Son of God (1 John 5:4-5).

In the movie *Smoke,* Dane locates his father, Cyrus, who abandoned him when he was born. The boy parks his car across the street from his father's house and watches him. Eventually Cyrus becomes irritated and walks over to ask Dane what he wants. In the heated exchange that follows, Dane is rebuked for staring at the hook prosthesis that replaces his father's left arm. Undaunted by his father's temper, Dane asks Cyrus how he lost his arm. Cyrus explains that years earlier he wrecked his car while driving drunk. The crash killed his wife and severed his arm. Cyrus believes he lost his wife and his arm because God was telling him to "mend his ways."

Dane asks his father if he has done that.

Cyrus replies, "No, but I keep trying."[31]

Cyrus expresses a false view of redemption that is held by millions — the view that a reconciliation with God is established by "mending one's ways." But the Bible teaches that redemption is only accomplished by God's acceptance of your repentant heart. He then establishes a relationship with you in which the Holy Spirit begins transforming you. It is this inner transformation that will result in real change — not a man-made "mending of one's ways" (Eph. 2:8-9; Luke 8:15).

Unfortunately, you, too, can mimic old Cyrus if you fail to trust God for spiritual transformation, and instead try to "mend your ways" by gung ho participation in outward "Christian" activities. But spirituality is not something you can lip sync. It has to be real to be effective. It has to be God working in you; otherwise it's just a mirage. Are *you* for real?

Sometimes it may seem difficult to get real in such an unreal world. Difficult and impossible if you're "Cyrus-ing" your way through life. That kind of tug-of-war approach can give the impression that the Christian life is more a struggle than a fulfillment, more depressing than hopeful. But to live and love Jesus by heart is to know victory over all things — personality glitches, poor discipline, selfishness, stupidity, and a long list of other ugly quirks (1 John 5:4-5). Authentic spirituality is knowing who you are in Christ, why you are here, what your calling is, and Who empowers you. It's not an act to get others to label you "spiritual"; it's the real you in action — the real you God fearfully and wonderfully made to shine for Him in your own unique way. And it's the purity of Jesus' spiritual DNA within you that empowers you to be your best self for God's glory (Ps. 139:13-14).

Often, you may look at another believer who is making a difference and say, "If only I could only be like Beverly." But here's a news flash: God doesn't want you to be like Beverly any more than He wants Beverly to be like you. He wants you to be like Jesus through your own unique personality, your own special gifts, your own charisma (Rom. 9:20). He wants you to be real for Him — to be transparent in an opaque world. He wants you to take off your mask and reveal the real thing — a unique life that knows Jesus by heart and lives it.

Think about Paul for a moment. Prior to his conversion on the Damascus Road, he was a powerful personality to be reckoned with. Zealous. Vigorous. Forthright. Committed to his cause of persecuting Christians. His personality was huge! It filled a room and caused people to take note. Enter the transforming power of God. God transformed Paul's heart; He gave Him the spiritual nature of Christ, but He didn't change Paul's personality. Instead, He changed Paul's focus. God took the unique traits He had given Paul at birth and redirected them at rebirth for His glory. Paul was still a powerful personality to be reckoned with. Zealous. Vigorous. Forthright. Committed to his cause. He still filled a room. But he had a higher calling. Paul was as real as they come and with his determination, his vigor, and his unswerving style, he was perfectly wired to accomplish what God had always intended for him to do: Stand and deliver the life-changing message of Jesus Christ.

What are *you* perfectly wired to be for God? "Nothing," you say? *Wrong answer.* Know this: There is no one else like you on the face of the earth. God designed it that way because He wants you to have His heart but to display it through your own unique personality, talents, and gifts. You are created and called by God to live your life as His unique servant. Edward Young aptly said, "We are born as originals but most of us die as copies."[32] Don't be a reproduction. You are God's unique child. He created you as one of a kind for a special calling. Be yourself for the glory of the One who made you so special.

List three "real-you" aspects of your personality that God can use to draw others to Jesus.

_____

_____

_____

For You formed my inward parts, You covered me in my mother's womb. I will praise you for I am fearfully and wonderfully made. Marvelous are Your works, And that my soul knows very well (Ps. 139:13-14, NKJV).

But indeed, O man, who are you to reply against God? Will the thing formed say to him who formed it, "Why have you made me like this?" (Rom. 9:20, NKJV).

Think of three ways God could use these unique qualities for His glory.

_____

_____

_____

God wants you to be transparent in an opaque world — to take off your mask and reveal the real thing: a life that lets Jesus shine through.

Check Point

Remember your commitment to heal a fractured relationship with a fellow believer? Note your progress.

_____

_____

_____

_____

How did reaching out to heal this relationship make you feel?

_____

_____

_____

_____

The new spiritual identity you have in Christ provides a new awareness of who you are. It makes you, at long last, comfortable in your own skin because that "skin" is His temple. It's time to come alive. You don't have to live like your mother wants you to or how the world tries to force you to — or even how you think "Christendom" expects you to. You are called to be real. God will live through you in a different way than He lives through others. Don't try to be like anyone else because God has specifically made you to draw certain people to Him that others cannot begin to magnetize.

In this unreal world, get real for God. Seek to deepen your relationship with Christ on a daily basis. It will solidify who you are. It will confirm Whose you are, and will forever change how you live.

Like Paul you now have a new purpose — a new direction in life. Be yourself but don't seek to serve yourself. Serve the One who set you free to be like Him. When you do that — when you get real different — your heart, a heart like His, will come shining through for His glory.

This Is Your Life: *Express Yourself*

What is your greatest obstacle to being who you are in Christ?

_____

_____

List two things you can begin to do today to overcome this obstacle.

_____

_____

A Moment with Jesus

"Today you will be with me in paradise" (Luke 23:43b).

It must have been difficult for Jesus to even utter those words aloud. Not because He didn't want to say them, but because every breath He labored to take came with excruciating pain. His body, beaten almost beyond recognition, baked and burned in the hot sun. Jesus trembled from the loss of blood; it pooled at the foot of the crude cross on which He hung. To catch a shallow, solitary breath required that He gather the courage and the strength to push himself up by His mangled feet, which caused the thick sharp spike to tear the flesh around it even more. His labored breaths rattled through His rapidly collapsing lungs and wheezed out through His brittle throat, which was closing fast due to dehydration. He could no longer wet His lips; they were cracked, bleeding, and covered with flies. He was dying and He knew it.

Yet Jesus didn't focus on Himself. Even then — in His darkest hour — when agony choked His soul, when the weight of the world crushed against Him, He turned His eyes to another's needs. He turned His head and His tender, forgiving heart to the thief hanging in agony next to Him. And He promised that repentant thief paradise.

That is love. Love that denies one's own pain so that another can find peace. Love that reaches out even when the human spirit is screaming, "Pull in! Pull in!" Love that offers: "My heart has plenty of room for you."

Jesus loved like that. And He wants you to love like that, too.

Jesus Loves Without End

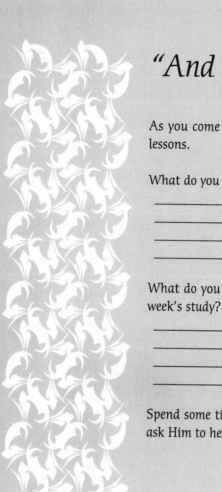

"And in Closing ..."

As you come to the close of this week's study, spend a few minutes reviewing the lessons.

What do you believe is the most important thing God has taught you this week?

_____

_____

_____

_____

What do you believe is the main action God would have you take based upon this week's study?

_____

_____

_____

_____

Spend some time in prayer. Thank God for speaking to you through your study and ask Him to help you put into life practice what you are learning.

Week 5
Enemies of Your Heart

While in elementary school Robertson McQuilkin was having a water pistol battle with one of his friends during recess. Just as Robertson pulled his trigger, the biggest bully in school walked by, and the water hit him right in the face. This dude was huge and could have easily turned Robertson into a pretzel with his bare hands, but instead he pulled a switchblade out of his pocket — and the chase was on.

Robertson began to run around and around the playground with the bully hot on his heels. As the bell rang Robertson bolted safely inside the building. But immediately following school, the big guy was waiting for him. For the next several days Robertson devised clever strategies to get around the bully and make it home. But finally he ran out of escape routes.

As he sat staring out his classroom window bemoaning his fate, he was stunned to see his father come walking down the sidewalk. Robertson ran out the back door, greeted him with great joy, and took him by the hand. As they rounded the corner together, Robertson waved at the bully, confident and courageous because of his father's presence.[33]

You, too, can have victory over the spiritual enemies in your life. But unlike Robertson's earthly father, your Heavenly Father is always with you. His Holy Spirit lifts you up when you're down, guides you when you're lost, cautions you when you're tempted, restores you when you fall, laughs with you when things go right, and weeps with you when things go wrong.

The goal of God's transforming grace is to overcome the barriers that stand in the way of your becoming the intimate companion of Jesus. This week you will take a close look at those spiritual enemies and the One who arms you for victory over them.

The goal of God's transforming grace is to overcome the barriers that stand in the way of your becoming the intimate companion of Jesus.

WEEK 5 AT A GLANCE

Day 1
Not Just the Devil's Own

Day 2
Know the Truth

Day 3
The Danger of Drifting and the Price of Rebellion

Day 4
Head Turners

Day 5
Armed and Ready

Day One: Not Just the Devil's Own

BY THE BOOK

"If the world hates you, keep in mind that it hated me first. If you belonged to the world, it would love you as its own. As it is, you do not belong to the world, but I have chosen you out of the world. That is why the world hates you. Remember the words I spoke to you: 'No servant is greater than his master.' If they persecuted me, they will persecute you also. If they obeyed my teaching, they will obey yours also. They will treat you this way because of my name for they do not know the One who sent me. If I had not come and spoken to them they would not be guilty of sin. Now, however, they have no excuse for their sin. He who hates me hates my

A little girl was in a very bad mood. She took out her frustrations on her younger brother, at first just teasing him, but eventually pulling his hair and kicking him in the shins. Finally he went crying to his mother, complaining about what his sister had done.

"Mary, why have you let Satan put it in your heart to tease your brother, pull his hair, and kick his shins?" asked her mother.

The little girl thought it over for a moment and then answered, "Well, Mother, maybe Satan did put it in my heart to tease Tommy and pull his hair, but kicking his shins was my own idea."[34]

This young girl was astute enough to acknowledge the devil's influence in her life, but she was honest enough to confess her own human role in her brother's torment. While the devil is an instigator, you play the pivotal role in making choices based on the heart of man rather than the heart of Jesus. What you do with your anger, hatred, and frustration is a choice of free will — not just an excuse to shout "the devil made me do it." The devil may applaud your bad choices, but he can't take all the credit for them. Some of the blame is yours and yours alone.

As a believer you'll find yourself in constant conflict with the flesh and many other enemies of your heart. But the world, the flesh, and the devil are enemies you'll encounter most every day of your life (John 15:18-27).

Take the world for example. The temptation to conform to its perspective can be like a strong whirlpool, sucking you down and under before you even know your feet are wet. Its pull represents everything God is against (1 John 2:16), and it'll give you loads of trouble. God's Word provides ample warning about this enemy, but it also includes a victory flag: *"I have told you these things, so that in me you may have peace. In this world you will have trouble. But take heart! I have overcome the world"* (John 16:33).

God is saying "Don't panic. Your victory over the world is sure as long as you love, trust, and obey Me." You are armed for battle against the world through prayer, Bible study, communion with Jesus, and relationships with other believers. But that means there's no room in your life for a secret storage closet for worldly loves. God says clean house or look out because His love and a love of the world can never inhabit the same heart. Believers just like you have discovered this truth throughout the centuries.

Jenny Lind was known as "The Swedish Nightingale" during her very successful career as an opera singer. She became one of the wealthiest artists of her time, yet she left the stage in the prime of her career. People speculated about the reason for her leaving, and most people wondered how she could give up so much applause, fame, and money. For her part, she seemed content to live in privacy by the sea.

One day a friend found her on the seashore, her Bible on her knees, looking out to the glorious glow of a sunset. As they talked, the friend asked Jenny, "How is it that you came to abandon the stage at the height of your success?"

She answered quietly, "When every day it made me think less of this (laying her finger on the Bible) and nothing at all of that (pointing to the sunset), what else could I do?"[35]

Think of the world's enticements: money, fame, lust, etc. The list is tempting. Do you secretly store a love of something the world offers? If so, complete the following as a pledge to God to "clean house." *Because* _____

_____

is preventing me from living Jesus by heart, I ask you, God, for victory over it in my life.

Now, if you think the world is a tough adversary, wait until you war against yourself — your old, crusty, "I-want-it-my-way" and "I'll-kick-and-scream-until-I-get-my-way" self. Self-centeredness is the bully that can run your spiritual life in circles and right into the ground — unless you battle it with God-centeredness. A heart like His doesn't say, "Satisfy me"; it says, "Not my will but Yours." It doesn't ask, "What do I get?" It asks, "What can I give?" You'll be empowered beyond belief when you lay down your wants and follow God's will as Jesus did. Jesus left the perfection of heaven to come to the blighted earth so that you could know God's very heart. Jesus confesses in John 6:38 that it was not His will but God's. Jesus left perfection to serve in pandemonium. A very unselfish choice indeed — and the model which you are given to live your life.

Think of your actions in the past few weeks. List two that were motivated by selfishness rather than servanthood.

_____

_____

If you had approached these moments with a servant's heart rather than a selfish one, what do you think you would have done differently? What spiritual battles might you have won?

_____

_____

Father as well. If I had not done among them what no one else did, they would not be guilty of sin. But now they have seen miracles, and yet they have hated both me and my Father. But this is to fulfill what is written in their Law: 'They hated me without reason.' When the Counselor comes, whom I will send to you from the Father, the Spirit of truth who goes out from the Father, he will testify about me. And you also must testify for you have been with me from the beginning"
(John 15:18-27).

For everything in the world — the cravings of sinful man, the lust of his eyes, and the boasting of what he has and does— comes not from the Father but from the world (1 John 2:16).

"For I have come down from heaven, not to do my will but to do the will of him who sent me" (John 6:38).

And no wonder, for Satan himself masquerades as an angel of light (2 Cor. 11:14).

The God of peace will soon crush Satan under your feet (Rom. 16:20).

THE MAIN THING

As your relationship with Christ grows, the influence of the world, the flesh, and the devil shrinks.

CHECK POINT

Stop and pray right now for the fellow believer that's "a fly in your soup." (See p. 76.)

And now for a word about Satan — a real devil of an adversary. He revels in putting as much distance between you and God as possible. But he's not the red-clad, pitchfork-toting troll that the world has cleverly cartooned him to be. Think of him that way and you're bound to get caught in one of his traps. The devil is slick and savvy. He doesn't wear a red suit; he wears blue jeans — so you'll be really comfortable with his sitting right there beside you, whispering in your ear. He knows the weak links in your arsenal. He's a "beaut" of an adversary (2 Cor. 11:14).

But he's dirt to God. He's powerless against the Father, who turns Satan's worst schemes into exhibitions for His own glory. Even Satan's grand performance — his use of human leaders and systems to condemn Jesus to death — resulted in the witness of God's eternal love for the lost. Satan's powerlessness to defeat Jesus is your assurance that you, too, can defeat him because you are a child of God (Rom.16:20).

This Is Your Life: The Devil in Blue Jeans

Think of the last time you were fooled by Satan. Did he kidnap you or did he casually slip right into that seat beside you and talk you into sin? Describe his most recent deception so that you will be reminded not to fall for that particular act again.

_____

_____

_____

_____

_____

_____

_____

_____

_____

_____

Day Two: Know the Truth

Ram Dass tells the story about God and Satan walking down the street. The Lord bends down, picks something up, and gazes at it glowing radiantly in His hand. Curious, Satan asks what it is. "This," answers the Lord, "is truth."

"Let me have that," says Satan. "I'll organize it for you."[36]

And Satan has been "organizing" (distorting) God's truth ever since. That's why it is so important for you to be deeply knowledgeable about the new identity you have in Christ — to understand the power of your new spiritual DNA, to understand the wisdom of God's truth, and to grasp the urgency of God's supreme calling to glorify Him by becoming like Jesus. A lack of knowledge in these areas will leave you confused, vulnerable, and drifting through life without a clear purpose. It will leave you asking "What do I do now?" (which by the way Satan views as an open invitation for deception) instead of confidently stating "My purpose is to know Jesus by heart so that I can glorify God."

A lack of knowledge of God's truth is a dangerous enemy to a growing relationship with Jesus Christ. Like a worm virus that slowly chews holes in computer programs, a lack of biblical knowledge — and thus a susceptibility to distorted knowledge — can ever so slowly halt your spiritual growth. Arming yourself to fight against misinformation is accomplished by studying the Word of God in depth and melding it with your mind and soul; so that when you do encounter distorted truth, warning lights go off just like a virus protector on your computer (Heb. 13:9a; 2 Pet. 1:12; 2 Pet. 3:17-18).

In his book *The Adequate Man*, Paul S. Rees discusses the pure truth that you need to know by heart. He calls it the "burning consciousness of Christ," which the Greek culture defined as "excellence." This excellence, this pure *truth* that the Gospel of Christ makes possible, is described in Philippians 4:8 as *"Whatever is true."* Rees explains it this this way:

> There is an order of truth and reality that is independent of us because it is grounded in God. Our business is not to conduct a Gallup Poll to learn what popular opinion may be or how it may be shifting. Our business is to make a norm, a standard, out of that reality that we see in God as He stands revealed in Jesus Christ. All truth may be a concern to us, but what is to lure us and lift us and command us is the truth that genuinely reflects the nature of God.[37]

Do not be carried away by all kinds of strange teachings (Heb. 13:9a).

So I will always remind you of these things, even though you know them and are firmly established in the truth you now have (2 Pet. 1:12).

Therefore, dear friends, since you already know this, be on your guard so that you may not be carried away by the error of lawless men and fall from your secure position. But grow in the grace and knowledge of our Lord and Savior Jesus Christ. To him be glory both now and forever (2 Pet. 3:17-18).

In his book *The High Calling* J. H. Jowett translates truth into street language: "Truth in a police court is correspondence with fact. Truth in the New Testament is correspondence with God."[38]

Are you seeking to correspond with God daily and deeply? Are you immersing yourself in the well of truth we call the Bible? Remember when you committed to learning new Scripture by memory so that the truths of the Bible become an inseparable part of you? List the verse references God is using to transform you spiritually.

_____

_____

_____

_____

_____

_____

If you ran out of verses before you ran out of lines, grasp this advice from C.S. Lewis: "The best safeguard against bad literature is a full experience of good literature."[39]

Likewise, the best protection against the bad information disseminated through the New Age movement, false religions, agnosticism, atheism, and the world in general is a full knowledge of what the truth really is. If your knowledge of biblical truth is shallow, you are extremely vulnerable to attacks by Satan in this area. He is adept at planting weeds of misinformation in a field of truth. You can be choked by weeds without even knowing it if you're not safeguarded by a full knowledge of truth. Claim victory over distortion by having the full experience of the truth that sets you free (1 Pet. 1:13-16).

And know this: Just as a knowledge of the truth sets you free, faith makes you strong — and keenly aware of God's presence.

After a 12-year-old boy asked God to forgive him of all the sins he had committed and accept him as His child, the boy's school friends questioned him about the experience.

"Did you hear God talk?" one asked.

"No," the boy said.

"Did you have a vision?" another asked.

"No," the boy replied.

"Well, how did you know it was God?" a third friend asked exasperated.

The boy thought for a moment and then said, "It's like when you catch a fish. You can't see the fish or hear the fish; you just feel him tugging on your line. I felt God tugging on my heart."[40]

There is a level of truth that defies the senses and objectivity. It is at that level that faith abounds. At the very heart of your faith is Jesus. As you grow in your faith through seeing God work in all areas of your life, you become capable of standing firm even in the darkest night, even when God is seemingly silent and the noise of Satan is deafening. You can just feel that God-tug (John 14:1).

But a lack of faith can leave you wavering just where Satan wants you — taking two steps forward and three steps back. A lack of faith will not only impede God's transforming process, it will wound your spirit and deter you from glorifying God. Do not let this enemy of your heart win. Live by faith in the One who has transformed your heart with His love. When you live the power of faith, Satan trembles. When you live by faith, just as Jesus did, there's no room in your life for Satan and his deceptions. He's left out in the cold flapping his arms in frustration (John 14:12a; 1 John 5:4).

Describe a time when your faith in God and His love saw you through when everything around you was bleak.

_____
_____
_____
_____
_____

How would you have handled the situation without God in your life?

_____
_____
_____
_____
_____
_____

Faith is the force that will carry you through many a spiritual battle. When you feel your faith weaken, strengthen it through prayer and by leaning on the support of other believers who bear witness to the truth that God never fails, never forsakes, and never falters in His love for you. He is the all knowing, all powerful Maker of heaven and earth. He can move mountains. And He loves you with all His heart. Rest in that knowledge and walk in the

"Do not let your heart be troubled. Trust in God, trust also in me" (John 14:1).

"I tell you the truth, anyone who has faith in me will do what I have been doing. He will do even greater things" (John 14:12a).

For everyone born of God overcomes the world. This is the victory that has overcome the world, even our faith (1 John 5:4).

faith that nothing can separate you from His amazing, empowering love.

CHECK POINT

What have you done this week to let Christ's presence come shining through you?

_____

_____

_____

_____

_____

_____

_____

This Is Your Life: Think About It

Name a subject about which you are very knowledgeable.

_____

_____

How much time and effort did you spend to become knowledgeable about this particular subject?

_____

_____

How does that investment compare with the time and effort you have invested in learning the truths of God's Word?

_____

_____

What adjustments, if any, do you need to make?

_____

_____

_____

_____

Day Three: The Danger of Drifting and the Price of Rebellion

Several men were preparing to canoe down a river. "You'll navigate the water just fine if you remember two things," said their guide: "*One.* The river can easily lull you into a false sense of security, so pay attention at all times. *Two.* Make sure you veer right when the river forks. The left fork is dangerous whitewater that's too powerful for these canoes. Don't be a daredevil. It'll cost you."

A few miles down the river, one man began relaxing as the sun kissed his face. The water was calm, so he closed his eyes for just a moment to let the canoe gently drift down the river. Soon he was fast asleep. Later he woke with a jolt. His canoe was stuck firmly on a sand bar. Try as he might, he could not dislodge it. He was forced to swim to the shore and hike ten miles back to base camp, two of which were a painstaking struggle through pitch darkness. He was hungry, thirsty, and had missed his ride home. Just as the guide had warned, his drift had cost him dearly.

Another man on the same excursion decided to prove his whitewater skills by ignoring the guide's warning and taking the left fork in the river. *I'll do this my way,* he thought to himself. *How tricky can the whitewater on a river this size be?* He soon found out. Moments later he hit churning whitewater that sucked him and his canoe under an outcrop of jagged rocks. He clawed his way to the surface only to have the churning water throw him into another pile of rocks, where he hung on, bruised and bleeding in the ice-cold water until rescue workers found him hours later.

Drifting and rebellion: two dangerous enemies of the heart. One is a slow unintentional detour that can leave your spiritual life stranded. The other is out-and-out disobedience to God, an "I'll do it my way" mind-set that has dire consequences.

The Bible warns you to "guard your heart" against drifting because it can happen so subtly. It's a slow ride off the course that God has charted for you. It can happen when you get lazy with your prayer life and Bible study — or a bit too busy with your daily life. You'll find yourself passing the days without growing any closer to God, drifting a long way from His will and not even being aware of it until something jolts you — a personal crisis, a concerned friend's confrontation, discipline from God (Heb. 2:1-3). Look back at your life. Can you see times when you drifted away from God without even

By the Book

Therefore, we must give the more earnest heed to the things we have heard, lest we drift away. For if the word spoken through angels proved steadfast, and every transgression and disobedience received a just reward, how shall we escape if we neglect so great a salvation, which at first began to be spoken by the Lord and was confirmed to us by those who heard Him (Heb. 2:1-3, NKJV).

There is a friend who sticks closer than a brother (Prov. 18:24b).

being aware of it? Describe a time like that.

_____

_____

_____

What jolted you back to awareness?

_____

_____

Inattentiveness leads to regression in your spiritual growth — and when your growth stops, your susceptibility to sin increases. It's vital that you pay attention and act on the things you have learned about the heart of your faith, the essence of spiritual transformation, and the visible signs of having a heart like that of Jesus. To safeguard yourself against future drifting, commit yourself to daily prayer, Bible study, and other spiritual exercises, but also ask a close spiritual friend to be your accountability partner — someone who will honestly confront you when you veer or just get plain lazy in your walk with Jesus (Prov. 18:24b).

Think of a fellow believer who might be a good accountability partner for you. Write that person's name below. Ask God to open the door for this individual to partner with you. Remember, iron sharpens iron, and an accountability partner will help keep you sharply focused on becoming like Jesus and thus glorifying God.

_____

While a drifting heart can strand your spiritual growth, a rebellious heart is a far graver matter for you as a believer. The Bible spotlights the pain and unhappiness that surrounded the Israelites when they shook their fists in the face of God and said, "We want to do it our way!" They got what their fists asked for — God's wrath and discipline (Heb. 3:7-11).

If you choose to rebel against God — to replace love, trust, and obedience with your own self-centered will, you're destined for trouble. Remember Jonah? His rebellion got him into a whale of a mess. When God told him to go to Nineveh and call the Assyrians to repentance, Jonah ran in the opposite direction. Granted, his self-centeredness was laced with a fear of the well-known cruelty of the Assyrians, but the bottom line was Jonah really didn't want the Assyrians to repent because he hated them, so he stamped his foot and said, "I'm not going!" His rebellion took him west toward

Tarshish when God wanted him to go east. Can't you just see God rolling His eyes as Jonah took off?

But Jonah's rebellion didn't just affect him; it wreaked havoc with the lives of the sailors on the ship Jonah boarded. God leaned back and sent a storm to tell Jonah, "You can run, but you can't hide." Although the compassionate sailors didn't want to toss Jonah overboard, they didn't have a choice: It was him or them. So in he went. But God in His mercy didn't let Jonah sink like a rock; he sent a large fish to swallow him; then He let Jonah think about the consequences of his rebellion for three days and nights in the stomach of that slimy fish. When the fish finally vomited Jonah up, he probably didn't smell good or feel chipper, but he headed straight for Nineveh — and the city repented.

Jonah learned the hard way that you can't say you love God if you aren't willing to do what He asks of you — no matter how hard it is. But he also learned that even the most rebellious heart can find forgiveness. Rebellion can prevent you from God's best and will always get you into a mess, but forgiveness brings you once again into His peace and rest.

If you battle the tendency to drift or rebel, ask God to strengthen you against these enemies of your heart. And continually remind yourself that drifting and rebellion aren't self-contained sins. They impact your loved ones, as well as fellow believers and the lost. Your actions will either hold the name of Jesus up or drag it down; you either draw others to Jesus or repel them from Him. Being a believer is indeed a serious responsibility.

Keep your heart focused on God and His leading — no matter how scary or "unlike you" it may seem. You'll avoid a whole lot of trouble. And for that your friends, family, and fellow believers will thank you.

This Is Your Life: He Ain't Heavy; He's Your Brother

Think of a fellow believer who seems to be drifting away from God? Write that person's initials. _____

Pray for that individual for five days. Ask God to give you (or another individual this person trusts) the wisdom to confront in love.

Now, think of someone you know who was once a dedicated believer who has rebelled against God and who is no longer living Jesus by heart. Will you commit to praying for this person every day for the next month?

THE MAIN THING

Drifting from God can leave your spiritual growth stranded; rebelling against God will get you into a whale of a mess.

CHECK POINT

Have you made a difference in the world this week? How?

_____
_____
_____
_____
_____
_____
_____
_____
_____

Day Four: Head Turners

As Martha pulled the fresh bread out of the oven, a trickle of sweat eased down her forehead. It was hot in the kitchen, but she didn't have time to step outside for a breath of cool air. She had dinner guests in the next room, and there was still much to do. Exasperated by the unchecked items on her "to-do" list, Martha looked around for her sister. The sound of Mary's gentle laughter drifted into the hot kitchen from the other room. *That's just great,* thought Martha. *Mary's in there having a grand old time while I'm in here slaving away.* She ducked her head around the door and tried to get Mary's attention. But Mary was totally focused on the guest of honor; she didn't even notice Martha. But the guest did.

With His attention now on her, Martha pleaded, "Master, don't you care that my sister has abandoned the kitchen to me? Tell her to lend me a hand." The guest's answer startled her: *"Martha, dear Martha, you're fussing far too much and getting yourself worked up over nothing. One thing is essential, and Mary has chosen it — it's the main course, and won't be taken from her"* (Luke 10:41-42, THE MESSAGE; see also Luke 10:38-40).

Martha was so distracted by having Jesus in her home that she failed to make room for Him in her heart. Mary, on the other hand, refused to let domestic details distract her from getting to know Jesus.

One of the most effective hindrances that Satan uses against you is distraction. With just a little prodding, Satan can veer you from your personal relationship with Jesus to activities that may or may not be good things. He can distract you from the victory you have in Jesus to fears about the future and regrets about the past. He can turn your heart from the grace and mercy of Christ to legalistic self-righteousness, from focus on God's glory to the pursuit of personal ambitions, from focus on your new vision of eternity to what you perceive must be done today.

Distraction has always been a staunch enemy of the heart. List two things that distract you from your relationship with Jesus.

_____

_____

What does Jesus want you to do? Just what Mary did: be totally dedicated to becoming like Him. Things that distract you from becoming like Him do not glorify God (Luke 9:62). God wants you to set aside your "to-do" lists and get to know His very heart just as Mary did. In essence He says,

"Seize the day! Don't put off knowing Me by heart. Don't gallop down rabbit trails. Don't let the unique gifts God has given you get out of proportion and in the way of your spiritual growth. I'm the main thing!"

Martha had a servant's head; but Jesus had to gently teach her how to have a servant's heart. Are you a Martha? Are you more focused on getting things done than becoming like Him? It's easy to get distracted when you live in a state of sensory-overload. But God wants you to slow down: *"Be still, and know that I am God"* (Ps. 46:10a).

THE MESSAGE puts it this way: *"Step out of the traffic! Take a long, loving look at me...."* When you take a long, loving look at Jesus in the Bible, you never see Him running frantically from town to town, stressed out because of the undone. Jesus was not performance-focused; He was people-focused. Even when His disciples tried to rush Him past small children who wanted His blessing, Jesus let His disciples know that He always had time, especially for little ones (Matt. 19:13-15). Jesus focused on people, not things. Do you?

If you're caught in the whirl of distractions or just overwhelmed by your self-created, inexhaustible "to-do" list — hit the brakes. Slow down. Be still. And get your focus back on Jesus Christ. God wants you to become like Jesus. Don't let anything or anyone distract you from making Him the center of your life. Don't let your fears get in the way. Don't let "spiritual activities" turn your head. Don't let anything or anyone keep you from knowing and loving Jesus by heart. Tomorrow those around you will not remember if you accomplished everything on your "to-do" list today, but they will remember you if you have a heart like His. And that's what matters most.

This Is Your Life: I Can See Clearly Now

What can you do today to gain victory over the distractions you listed earlier?

_____

_____

_____

Ask your spiritual mentor to "point check" you for victory over these distractions. Use the following verse as your call to arms:

"And this I say for your own profit, not that I may put a leash on you, but for what is proper, and that you may serve the Lord without distraction" (1Cor. 7:35, NKJV).

Then little children were brought to Jesus that he might put his hands on them and pray for them. But the disciples rebuked those who brought them. Jesus said, "Let the little children come to me, and do not hinder them for the kingdom of heaven belongs to such as these." When he had placed his hands on them, he went on from there (Matt. 19:13-15).

THE MAIN THING

Distractions leave your life in wasted fractions. Focus on Jesus.

CHECK POINT

Recite Romans 12:1-2. This Scripture appears on page 7 of this book.

Day Five: Armed and Ready

There are a lot of enemies out to short-circuit your desire to know and love Jesus by heart. But the Christian life is not a precarious trek along a high-wire, requiring skill, luck, and the right circumstances. God is your fortress, your protector — and He has provided everything you need to be armed and ready for all the enemies of the heart — Satan, the flesh, the world, lack of knowledge of the Scriptures, lack of faith, drifting, rebellion, and distraction.

But you must be an active participant in the battle. Ephesians 6:10-18 is full of proactive commands spoken directly to you: *Be strong. Put on. Stand firm. Take up. Be alert. Pray.* This means that, just like a soldier, you have to check your battle-readiness daily. Leave any part of your protection off and you become an easy target for trouble. The enemy will always attack the weakest flank.

So, what does the battle gear of a transformed heart consist of? First, arm yourself with the "belt of truth," which requires that you be totally honest in everything you do and say. No lies — white, black, or gray should fall out of your mouth. Remember, lies weaken your defenses because they require constant upkeep. The truth always stays in place.

Next, you must protect yourself with the "breastplate of righteousness," which is an unswerving commitment to moral purity. More believers have stumbled in this area than Christendom would care to admit. This particular piece of armor must be solid and must be reinforced daily with prayers for the strength and foresight to say "no", even when that seductive voice inside your head is whispering "yes."

Your next protection against the enemies of your transformed heart is an aggressive offense. A "readiness to share the gospel" reminds Satan of his ultimate defeat while it glorifies God. Each time you share the gospel you become more empowered to do so again.

Keeping a calm head in fierce battle is the sign of a strong, confident person. The Bible talks about the "helmet of salvation" being vital armor because it helps you make decisions based on a strong assurance of your new identity in Christ. You know *Whose* you are, therefore you have a spiritual strength that a lost person does not have.

A deep knowledge of the Word of God can take you through anything Satan can fling at you — be it temptation or distortion of the truth. This "sword of the spirit" makes a point that Satan can't deny.

As a well-armed believer you also have the "shield of faith," which can repel lots of missiles, not to mention a few rocks. A strong faith in God and His ultimate power constantly reminds you that the victory over all the things that hammer your defenses every day is actually already won because of Jesus' death on the cross.

Finally, the most powerful offensive weapon of all is readily accessible: *Prayer.* The Bible tells you in 1 Thessalonians 5:17 (KJV) to *"Pray without ceasing."* Romans 12:12 admonishes you to continue *"steadfastly in prayer."* Philippians 4:6 entreats you to *"Be anxious for nothing but in everything by prayer and supplication, with thanksgiving, let your requests be made known to God."* The New Testament overflows with directives to pray. The importance of prayer is unquestionable. Its power is indisputable. Your open access to God is invincible. And God will answer your requests to part seas, move mountains, and make Satan cringe. Prayer changes things. Never forget that.

Fighting the good fight isn't always easy; the enemies of your heart are experienced warriors. But when God is on your side there's nothing to be afraid of. He is indeed a mighty conqueror.

This Is Your Life: War Zone

Of all the enemies of the heart, which one would you say represents your greatest threat?

_____

Why do you think you are most susceptible to this one?

_____

_____

_____

Stop now and ask God to strengthen you against this enemy. What Scripture verse will you claim as your fight song against this enemy of your heart? Write that verse and memorize it.

_____

_____

_____

_____

_____

extinguish all the flaming arrows of the evil one. Take the helmet of salvation and the sword of the Spirit, which is the word of God. And pray in the Spirit on all occasions with all kinds of prayers and requests. With this in mind, be alert and always keep on praying for all the saints (Eph. 6:10-18).

The Main Thing

As a well-armed believer you are prepared for victory over the enemies of your heart.

CHECK POINT

There are many voices in the body of Christ with one calling to glorify God. Are you singing with them or causing discord? (See pp. 74-76.)

A Moment with Jesus

And He said to them, "Why did you seek Me? Did you not know that I must be about My Father's business?" (Luke 2:49, NKJV).

After a frantic search, Mary and Joseph found 12-year-old Jesus in the temple doing exactly what God wanted Him to do — His Father's business. Jesus by His very heart was obedient to God and the mission His Father had given Him to do on earth. Throughout the Gospels we see that Jesus did not stray from this, even though many people — even His disciples — often tried to redirect His focus. But Jesus pressed on. He stayed true to God's mission for Him. So true that on the cross the last words of Jesus said volumes about Him:

"It is finished" (John 19:30).

Jesus finished well. His life was like the seamless robe He wore. From Bethlehem to Calvary, He lived without sin or shame. He was faithful to God's calling every day of His life, totally focused on what God placed Him on earth to do. He died with a triumphant shout of victory. The work of redemption, which was the object of His earthly life, had been completed and the plan of salvation established. Jesus finished. And He finished well.

Few can look at the life they've lived and say, "My job is finished." Instead, most are like the brilliant composer Franz Schubert, who died at age 31, leaving as a parable of human life his unfinished symphony — a breathtaking melody begun well but left forever longing for its final, exquisite strains.

To know and love Jesus by heart is to be obedient to God's calling. Are you focused on what God has put you on this earth to do for His glory — to be just like Jesus?

God wants Jesus to live out His life through you. He wants you to finish well. Do not become an unfinished symphony. Surrender your life totally to God's calling, so that when your life on this earth reaches its end you, too, can say, "It is finished."

Jesus Was Obedient to God

"And in Closing ..."

As you come to the close of this week's study, spend a few minutes reviewing the lessons.

What do you believe is the most important thing God has taught you this week?

_____

_____

_____

_____

What do you believe is the main action God would have you take based upon this week's study?

_____

_____

_____

_____

Spend some time in prayer. Thank God for speaking to you through your study and ask Him to help you put into life practice what you are learning.

Week 6
Your Urgent Heart

Your transformed heart must now become an intensely urgent one.

Ngo Thi Lam, phonetically and most undeservedly pronounced *Naughty Lamb*, was a small puff of a girl. As a tender victim of the chaos and horror of the Vietnam war, she was left abandoned outside one of the crowded orphanages in the Mekong Delta. By a miracle of God she was seen at six months of age by U.S. Air Force Captain Robert Allen Peck, who had a wife and sons living back in the States. Touched to his soul by the delicate waif, he wrote to his good wife Phyllis, living half a world away, and they decided to adopt Naughty Lamb.

While the decision to adopt the fragile little girl was an easy conviction of the heart, the process was a bureaucratic nightmare. But finally, 13 months later, Naughty Lamb was headed for the States, held in the temporary but protective arms of journalist Bob Considine. With the war in high gear, any person traveling back to the States (or any other country for that matter) was not permitted to travel unaccompanied. Rosemary Taylor, the tenacious head of the orphanage, made sure of that. She'd place one of her passport-bearing orphans in a traveler's arms to deliver to the waiting arms of the child's new parents. Rosemary wouldn't take no for an answer.

Naughty Lamb, a quiet little doll with the most luminous dark eyes, made no sound as she stared at everything around her during the flight. She stole the heart of everyone on board that plane, and Bob Considine felt like a proud papa. An hour out of Tokyo, Bob began playing a game that Naughty Lamb liked. She would pull a light blanket over her face and then reach out from under it to expose the little finger of her left hand. Bob would kiss it, pull back the blanket, and find her smiling ever so happily.

But once, when he pulled back the blanket, Naughty Lamb was not smiling. She was silently weeping. Great tears were running down her doll cheeks. Bob rang for the stewardess, and when she came he asked what was wrong, why the baby was crying but making no crying sound. The stewardess, an old hand at this phenomenon, said a most chilling thing:

"I've seen this before with these kids," she said tenderly. "The reason they don't make any sound when they cry is because they learned a long time ago that nobody will come."

With his heart in tatters, Bob Considine gently held Naughty Lamb's

cheek close to his, and he and the fragile waif of a senseless war had a nice cry together.[41]

Silent weepers. Your world is full of them. Lost souls who feel abandoned. People who have ceased to cry out loud because no one has responded to them with God's love in the past. Now they weep silently, convinced there is no hope. Convinced no one cares. Convinced that this is all there is to life.

These silent souls are waiting for you and your transformed heart to cry with them and then lead them to the tender arms of Jesus Christ. You live in a world where needs are kept silent, hidden from view. You must look with your heart to see the cry that often is not uttered. In fact, God has placed in your new heart the drive to seek out and help those that are weeping silently, those that are separated from God by their sins. It is part of your new spiritual DNA. This urging, this intense calling flows from the very heart of Jesus:

"When he saw the crowds, he had compassion on them, because they were harassed and helpless, like sheep without a shepherd. Then he said to his disciples, 'The harvest is plentiful but the workers are few. Ask the Lord of the harvest, therefore, to send out workers into his harvest field'" (Matt. 9:36-38).

God has given you a new heart that propels you to reach out to the lost — to touch their pain and despair with the healing grace of God. Can you see the tears of those around you who have cried out for so long without response? Can you feel the despair of those who have tried everything to find peace, happiness, and love but remain alone? They are calling out in the only way they know how — with silent tears. Will you reach out with the heart of Jesus and show them that their cries are heard and that there is hope for a brighter tomorrow?

Last week you learned about spiritual enemies, those forces that seek to prevent you from knowing Jesus by heart. This week you will learn why time is of the essence. Why your transformed heart must now become an intensely urgent one.

They weep in silence because their cries have not been heard. What will be the response of your heart?

Day One: Hear the Call and Answer It

The bitter wind would not give up. It pushed her, beat her, nailed her brutally to the ground. There was no escape from its wrath. Not for her. Not that day. She was far from any shelter, far from any hope for herself. She knew that. As sure as the icy wind beat against her she knew that.

But she refused to believe there was no hope for the child she had just given birth to in the snow. For him, her very heart, there must be hope. As the ice began to freeze her breath and knot her fingers, she removed all of her outer clothes and wrapped her newborn son in the layered folds. Then she drew him close to her heart as she huddled on the ground, sheltering him from the wind, the snow, and the cold as best she could, giving him the legacy of her body's warmth as she died.

Hours later some men heard soft whimpering coming from a lump in the snow. Underneath the frozen body of the young mother, the baby boy survived in the echo of his mother's warmth. He was rushed to a hospital and was later adopted by a missionary couple whose hearts were touched by the vision of a mother who gave all so that her son could live.

Years later, on the boy's 16th birthday, the couple took him to the grave of his mother, where he asked to be left alone. When the couple returned they found the young man had removed all his outer clothes, placed them on his mother's snow-covered grave, and lay face down on top of it. He was pledging to his mother — who had given her all so that he might live — that he, too, would give all so that others might live.[42]

This young man heard the call. Not in his head but in his heart — a call so strong it could not be ignored. As he traced his fingers over his mother's name carved on the headstone, he knew that she had written his own name on her heart. He knew that she had loved him above all else. And that she had given all because of that love. In his heart the boy knew he could do no less. He would spend his life telling others about the two who gave all so that he might live — His mother and His Lord, Jesus Christ.

Jesus gave His all for you. He laid down His life and covered your sins with His blood. Why? Because He loves you with all His heart. Now you are His legacy on this earth. In this year, on this day, will you strip off all the layers of excuses you have used for not giving your all to Him and begin to truly live your life so that others might also know of the One who gave all for them (John 13:1b)?

In John 13:12-17 we see Jesus set the example of compassionate love and servanthood by washing the feet of His disciples. He didn't do this to be nice. He did it for a greater purpose: to extend His mission on earth after He was gone. The men whose feet He so humbly washed were to move into the world serving God, serving each other, and serving all people to whom they took the message of salvation. Jesus set the example by living the example before them. No act was too lowly for Him. He demonstrated total commitment. He demonstrated unconditional love.

What excuses for not being totally committed to sharing the love of Christ do you need to ask God to strip off today? List those below. Ask God to forgive you for letting thin excuses keep you from answering His call. Pray for victory over these excuses.

_____

_____

_____

_____

When God accepted you as His child, you were responding to His first call — to place everything you had ever done wrong at the feet of the only One who could forgive you and set you free to become everything you never thought you could be. It was a miraculous gift that can never be repaid.

Now, every time your feet hit the floor in the morning, His feet hit the floor in front of you. And you hear the second call — to be like Him — to follow in His footsteps, whether those steps lead you to the mountaintop or to the muddy cesspools of life.

Psalm 23 is the blanket of promise that wraps you in its warmth as you take each step of your life. It promises that He leads you each step of the way. He never tells you to go on without Him; He never leaves your side or lets go of your hand. He is with you always, your constant and ever-close companion.

To bring the reality of His abiding presence home, fill in the blanks of Psalm 23 with your name and then read the passage aloud.

"The Lord is _____ shepherd, _____ shall not be in want. He makes _____ lie down in green pastures, he leads _____ beside quiet waters, he restores _____ soul. He guides _____ in paths of righteousness for his name's sake. Even though _____

walk[s] through the valley of the shadow of death, _____ will fear no evil, for you are with _____; your rod and your staff they comfort _____ . You prepare a table before _____ in the presence of _____ enemies. You anoint _____ head with oil; _____ cup overflows. Surely goodness and mercy will follow _____ all the days of _____ life, and _____ will dwell in the house of the Lord forever" (Ps. 23).

What a resounding promise! What empowerment! Because of the sacrifice of Christ, you are forever guided and guarded by God. Take joy in that. Take comfort in that. And be forever thankful. Then valiantly answer the Kingdom call — the call of the Great Commission that forbids you to keep His great love to yourself but commands you to go into the world and draw others to Christ (Matt. 28:19-20). To go so that they, too, "will dwell in the house of the Lord forever."

Your forgiven heart bears witness that you have answered the call of the cross; your transformed life bears witness that you have answered the call to be like Jesus. Now your urgent heart must answer the call of The Great Commission. Will you? Will you lay down your life as Jesus did? Will you lay down your life as the young mother did? Will you lay down your life as her son did? Will you?

This Is Your Life: Some Gave All

Think of a person in your life who sacrificed greatly for you. It might be a family member, a friend, or a total stranger. Write that person's name.

_____

Take the time today to contact that person and express your heart-felt gratitude for their loving sacrifice. If you are unable to contact this person due to death, write a letter to them straight from your heart and keep it in your Bible as a reminder of someone who gave all for you. May it be a constant reminder for you to give all for others.

THE MAIN THING

Daily you must answer the call to give your all so that others might come to know Jesus as you do.

CHECK POINT

Think of someone you know who needs to know that Jesus gave His all for him or her. Write that person's name here and talk to them about Christ this week.

_____

Day Two: The Task Won't Be Easy

BY THE BOOK

I can do everything through him who gives me strength (Phil. 4:13).

It is God who arms me with strength and makes my way perfect (2 Sam. 22:33).

The Lord is my strength and my shield; my heart trusts in him, and I am helped. My heart leaps for joy and I will give thanks to him in song. The Lord is the strength of his people, a fortress of salvation for his anointed one. Save your people and bless your inheritance; be their shepherd and carry them forever (Ps. 28:7-9).

Missionaries Von and Marge Worten were asked to minister to a tribe living in a high, remote area of Asia. The decision to embrace this opportunity was easy. Getting to the remote village was another matter. It meant climbing up a 4,000 foot mountain, then down the other side to a river valley, over the side of another mountain and back down to the river valley, then up for 5,000 feet. Five hours into the trip, the weary climbers were still below the crest of the first mountain. Marge collapsed under a tree, too exhausted to sob, but tears of despair seeped out of her eyes and ran down into her ears. As she lay there engulfed in hopelessness, she told God, "Lord, what am I going to do? I can't go on; I can't go back. I can't even get up. What am I going to do?"

God answered her as clearly as if He had spoken with an audible voice: "Marge, I climbed Calvary for you." And at that moment Marge knew that God was going to get her up those mountains to the village. The rest of the trip was an experience of God's grace. Marge learned step by agonizing step that God's grace is sufficient, but that grace doesn't necessarily take away pain. Grace came in the form of her husband Von's walking stick. He literally pulled her up the side of the mountain as she hung onto the stick. Going downhill she rested her hands on Von's shoulders and placed her foot wherever he had just put his. Grace came through knowing that people were praying for her. Grace came through God bringing to Marge's mind every verse she had ever known dealing with God's strength and power (Phil. 4:13; 2 Sam. 22:33; Ps. 28:7-9).

As they finally neared the remote village, Marge could hear the villagers singing in the distance: *"Come and go with me to my Father's house where there is joy, joy, joy!"* Today, when Marge hears that tune, her mind rolls back to the night when under a star-spangled sky she wearily, thankfully, achingly, and yes, joyfully entered the Himalayan village with the knowledge that it was the sheer grace of God that had gotten her there.

And what awaited her there was well worth the intense agony of the struggle. God gifted her with hundreds of new believers who were praying with aching hearts for someone to teach them about Jesus. And because God had uniquely prepared Von and Marge to teach the truths of God's Words verbally to new believers who had never seen a Bible, the transformation of these thirsty Christians was miraculous. During the next few days many things happened that made the journey worth more than the pain. But what

Marge thanks God most for is the proven, bone-deep assurance that He who climbed Calvary gives grace for anything He leads His children to do – even though it may be through a valley of agony.[43]

The path God calls you to is not an easy one. Often it will seem impossible, too large a task for you. It is in those moments of your *inability* that you will most clearly see God's unlimited *ability* to carry you and use you even when you think it's impossible. *The Message* brings the reality of this into focus in Matthew 5:3: *"You're blessed when you are at the end of your rope. With less of you there is more of God and His rule."*

Think of a time when you were at the end of your rope, when the task seemed too daunting or the pain too great. Describe that incident.

_____

_____

How did you find the power and the strength to go on?

_____

_____

What did this victory in the midst of seemingly insurmountable odds teach you about the power of God and the true source of strength?

_____

_____

Perhaps you are now facing a difficult task. Claim the promises found in 1 Chronicles 16:11; Psalm 46:1; and 2 Corinthians 4:6-9 as God's personal encouragement to you to press on through the wind and the rain. Be empowered by Him as you seek to follow Christ through the mountains and valleys of life.

And know this. Sometimes following God's call requires more mental adaptability than physical or emotional strength. Just ask Wilson Talmage, a missionary to the natives of the upper regions of the Nile. Wilson's old Volkswagen bus permitted him to travel, in one hour, an astonishing eight or nine times further than the fastest person could manage on foot. It was from behind the wheel of such a battered vehicle that Wilson made his 120-mile circuit through the villages under his care. His mission coworkers loved to see the dust cloud accompanying the little van, for along with news and warm smiles Wilson would sometimes bring suitcases full of bright red Washington apples — true opulence by bush standards.

Blessed are the poor in spirit for theirs is the kingdom of heaven (Matt. 5:3).

Look to the Lord and his strength; seek his face always (1 Chron. 16:11).

God is our refuge and strength, an ever-present help in trouble (Ps. 46:1).

For God, who said, "Let light shine out of darkness," made his light shine in our hearts to give us the light of the knowledge of the glory of God in the face of Christ. But we have this treasure in jars of clay to show that this all-surpassing power is from God and not from us. We are hard pressed on every side, but not crushed, perplexed but not in despair; persecuted, but not abandoned; struck down, but not destroyed (2 Cor. 4:6-9).

THE MAIN THING

In your inability you will most clearly see God's unlimited ability to use you —even when you think it's impossible.

CHECK POINT

Reread Psalm 23 aloud, inserting your name. (See pp. 106-107.) Make it a point to read it once a week as affirmation of God's continuing guidance of your life.

But one day, disaster struck. The forward gears in the bus wouldn't grab, and the VW made about as much progress as a beached whale. Wilson scratched his head, considered his predicament, and prayed. The vehicle God provided had faithfully bounced him over many miles to bring the gospel to others. And the job was far from done. Wilson wasn't going to let a little thing like a balky transmission keep him from his appointed rounds. Grateful for the one gear that still functioned, the indomitable Talmage Wilson completed his 120-mile circuit — in reverse. Thinking out of the box may have given him a bit of a neck cramp, but it was a small price to pay. His job was not done and if driving in reverse was the only way to get it done, then so be it![44]

Your job is not done either. But are you allowing unexpected hitches in life to keep you from your appointed rounds? Think of something you need to do for Christ that you have put on hold because things didn't go as planned. Describe that "something."

_____
_____
_____

Now, ask God to show you an out-of-the-box solution to this barrier — even if it may be a bit of a pain in the neck. Write your creative solution.

_____
_____
_____
_____

There's no verse in the Bible that says what God has called you to do will be easy. But the Bible is full of verses that promise He will give you strength when you are weary — and creativity when you're confronted by a barrier. Rest in the truth that He will carry you through the tough times. Get a kick out of the fact that He will spark you with creative ways to overcome obstacles if you'll just ask.

This Is Your Life: *Creative Coworkers*

Share your God-given creativity. Help someone else be open to a creative solution to what may seem like an insurmountable problem. Remember, two heads are better than one.

Day Three: Know What's at Stake

Alvin Reid, professor of evangelism at Southeastern Baptist Seminary shared the following story in a meeting of the American Society for Church Growth.

> The old German man stood before the group with tears streaming down his lined face. "I lived in Germany during the Nazi Holocaust. I considered myself a Christian. I attended church since I was a small boy. We had heard the stories of what was happening to the Jews, but like most people today in the United States, we tried to distance ourselves from the reality of what was taking place. What could anyone do to stop it?
>
> "A railroad track ran behind our small church, and each Sunday morning we would hear the train whistle from a distance, followed by the clacking of the wheels moving over the track. We became disturbed when one Sunday we heard cries coming from the train cars as they passed by. We grimly realized that the train was carrying Jews to concentration camps. They were like cattle in those cars. Week after week, that train whistle would blow. We would dread the sound of those old clacking wheels because we knew that Jews would begin to cry out as they passed our church. It was terribly disturbing. We felt we could do nothing to help those poor miserable people, yet their screams tormented us. We knew exactly at what time the whistle would blow and we decided that the only way to keep from being so disturbed by the cries was to start singing our hymns. By the time the train came rumbling past the church yard, we were singing at the top of our voices. If some of the screams reached our ears, we would sing a little louder until we could hear them no more. Years have passed and no one talks about it any more, but I can still hear that train whistle in my sleep.
>
> "And I can still hear those people crying out for help."

May Dr. Reid's closing prayer at that meeting be your own prayer today:

"God, forgive all of us who call ourselves Christians, yet do nothing to intervene when others cry for help. In our studies, our demographics, our statistics, our writings, our seminars, all of which are wonderful, let us never, never, never miss the passion of God and the basis of what we do — the cross of Christ. Christ came to save sinners. He asks us to not be silent, but to tell them."[45]

Who is crying out to you for help today? Is it a neighbor? An elderly person in a nursing home? A relative? A single parent struggling to be two people? A young boy without a father? A young girl without a mother? Write the names of those whose cries you have recently heard.

_____

_____

_____

If you have ignored their cries ask yourself why and write those reasons.

_____

_____

_____

Now, know this truth. You may be the only person God has put into place to reach these individuals for Jesus. If you do not listen to their cries and speak the love language of Jesus, these people, entrusted by God into your care, may spend eternity separated from Him.

Is that what you want to happen? Do you think that's what God wants to happen? Absolutely not. He loves those souls just as much as He loves you. Are you afraid they will reject you? Then think of this: Imagine for a moment the roles were reversed and you were in their place, wouldn't you want someone to reach out to *you* with the love of Christ? Wouldn't you want someone to show *you* how to spend eternity with God?

You are called to break the silence. For if you don't, the silence will condemn many to an eternity of hopelessness. Shut off from God. Forever (Rev. 20:15).

Granted, it can be difficult to share your faith with others. But as the old German man learned, it is harder not to. You must take that risk. Because the option that is left is no option at all.

Granted, it can be difficult to share your faith with others. Seventeen-year-old Cassie Bernall, who died in the Columbine High School shootings in Littleton, Colorado, confronted the fear of sharing her faith as few have. When Dylan Klebold and Eric Harris held their weapons in her face and asked, "Cassie, do you believe in God?" the girl was faced with the most difficult of choices: to deny her faith and possibly live or to profess her love of God and most certainly die.

According to some reports, before Cassie became a Christian she was considered an "outcast" herself. But when Cassie asked Jesus to replace the darkness in her life with His light, everything changed. She became like Jesus. Her family witnessed her life change. Her friends were amazed by it. Her teachers commented on it. And Dylan Klebold and Eric Harris watched it—and took note. When they spotted Cassie in the school library and asked her if she believed in God, the two killers knew the answer. Cassie's life had already lived the answer out loud. What Cassie could not have known when she verbally responded, "Yes, I believe in God," was that her testimony would be heard around the world long after the sound of the fatal gunshots ceased. But before she uttered her final words Cassie did know, without a doubt, that no bullet could separate her from the love of God or the eternal life He promised her when she gave her life to Him. With everything at stake, Cassie gave her life for the name of Jesus—just as Jesus had given His life for her.

The world was forever changed because of the death of Jesus, and now more lives have been changed because a 17-year-old girl could not—would not—remain silent about her faith in God. Even in the face of certain death.

Look at those around you. Realize what's really at stake. Whose eternity are you risking with your silence? It is time to speak. Time to be heard. Time to stand up for Jesus. No matter the cost. Whose eternity are you risking with your silence?

This Is Your Life: *Jesus in You*

Think of those individuals you listed on the previous page. Stop and pray for each of those people now. Then pick up the phone, walk across the street, jump in your car — or do whatever it takes to begin reaching out to these people who are crying out for your help. You may be the only glimpse of Jesus they ever see.

THE MAIN THING

You are called to speak in the silence. For if you do not, your silence will condemn many to an eternity of hopelessness, shut off from God's love, from God's light. Forever.

CHECK POINT

Describe how your relationship with Jesus is stronger today than it was when you began this study.

———————————

———————————

———————————

———————————

———————————

———————————

———————————

Day Four: Know How the Story Ends

BY THE BOOK

"Then you will know the truth and the truth will set you free.... So if the Son sets you free you will be free indeed" (John 8:32, 36).

You have been set free from sin and have become slaves to righteousness (Rom. 6:18).

It is for freedom that Christ has set us free. Stand firm then and do not let yourselves be burdened again by a yoke of slavery (Gal. 5:1).

"However, I consider my life worth nothing to me, if only I may finish the race and complete the task the Lord Jesus has given me — the task of testifying to the gospel of God's grace" (Acts 20:24).

A minister once gave a sermon with an empty bird cage as the lone prop. He told the story of a young boy who'd once owned the bird cage and its occupants. Spying the young boy and his birds an old Pastor asked, "Where'd you get those birds, son?"

"I caught 'em," the boy replied.

"What you going do with them?" the kind Pastor asked.

"Play with 'em," replied the boy.

"Then what are you going do with them?" asked the Pastor.

"I'll probably feed 'em to the cats."

"How much will you take for them?" asked the wise Pastor.

"Oh, you don't want these mister; they're just field birds," said the boy.

"How much?" insisted the Pastor.

Soon a deal was reached and the bird cage full of birds was given to the old Pastor. He took the cage and walked around the corner into an alley, and when nobody was looking, he set the birds free.

The minister's sermon continued.

Once God met Satan leaving the Garden of Eden with a cage full of people.

"Where'd you get those people?" God asked.

"I caught 'em," replied Satan.

"What are you going to do with them?" God asked.

"I'm gonna play with 'em," Satan snapped.

"Then what are you going to do with them?"

"I'm gonna kill 'em," spat Satan.

"How much will you take for them?" asked God.

Satan pondered for just a moment then whispered, "All the tears you can cry, and all the blood you can bleed."

A deal was struck and the cage exchanged hands. And when nobody was looking, on a quiet night in a lonely manger, God set the humans free (John 8:32, 36; Rom. 6:18; Gal. 5:1).[46]

Freedom. That's what you have. That is what was born in a manger and what was paid for on the cross — freedom to live and reign forever with Jesus. What a future you now have! Psychics may try to predict the future. But as a child of God you *know* the future. The road ahead may be long with lots of winding turns. But you know where it ends: God will reign. Love will conquer hate. Light will dispel darkness. And you will live for all eternity with Him. The yearning of your heart for perfection will finally be satisfied. The vision for eternity will become the reality of eternity.

The victory is assured. All you must do is finish the race (Acts 20:24). You have spent the last six weeks discovering that your purpose for living is to glorify God; to love, trust, and obey His calling so that others will come to know Him, too. It is a high — and often a hard — calling. But now that you know that Jesus is the very heart of God and that God wants you to be just like Jesus, you are empowered by God to live as Jesus lived. To love as Jesus loved. To trust as Jesus trusted. And to obey as He obeyed.

God has changed and will continue to change you from the inside out for His glory and honor. *"So here's what I want you to do, God helping you: Take your everyday, ordinary life — your sleeping, eating, going-to-work, and walking around life — and place it before God as an offering"* (Rom. 12:1-2, *The Message*). Fix your attention on God. And watch Him transform you into a walking miracle.

Today is indeed the first day of the rest of your life. May it be a life that lives Jesus by heart.

This Is Your Life: Teach the World to Sing

Pretend for a moment that you are tone deaf. That when you sing in the shower the ceramic tiles beg for more soap scum to block the noise. Then imagine that, miraculously, when you woke up this morning you had the most exquisitely beautiful singing voice ever heard. A voice that makes Pavarotti sound like a frog. A voice that is as close to heaven as you can get on this earth. But you decide to never use it. To never sing a note. What a shame, what a loss, what a sin that would be. The world would weep.

Your transformed heart has a new voice. And it's time for you to sing. Your voice has the message that can transport others to heaven. To never sing with the new voice He has given you will be a shame, a loss, a sin. The world will weep if you remain silent.

You are the voice of Jesus. Sing His song.

THE MAIN THING

God's ultimate victory over all evil is certain. And knowing how the story ends makes it easier to begin each day.

CHECK POINT

Go back through the study and reread all the "check points." You will realize just how far you have come during the last six weeks. Write down three new "Check Points" you would like to challenge yourself with in the coming weeks.

_____

_____

_____

_____

_____

_____

Day Five: Become God's Emissary

Ralph Hodge climbed onto the small electric vehicle that would drag him and his guide down a two-mile, 40-inch-high crease inside one of Kentucky's coal mines.

"When my grandfather worked the mines, he had to trust his life to a canary," the miner said. As the tunnel crowded around them, Ralph turned to look at the miner in the murky darkness. "A canary?" he queried nervously. With a grim nod the miner said, "Back then a miner's life wasn't much longer than a bird's song — if the singing stopped."

He explained that a great danger in the mines is "firedamp," a highly combustible, odorless mixture of methane gas and air created by the decomposition of coal. As he and Ralph moved through the mine he showed Ralph the modern devices designed to detect methane gas today. Before such technology existed, it was a practice to keep a canary deep in the mines — where it would sing its heart out, regardless of the noise and activity. However, if methane gas, undetectable by miners, began to build up in the shafts — the canary would stop singing. In the eerie stomach-knotting silence that followed, the miners knew they had only a brief window of opportunity to escape before the gas build-up exploded. If the canary died, the opportunity for escape died too.[47]

That same kind of eerie, stomach-knotting silence can be heard in the world today. In spite of the unprecedented peace and prosperity of our time, low-grade pessimism and fear for the future hang like a dark cloud. There is frustration, pent-up restlessness, and a sense of confusion, uncertainty — even dread. The prevailing interest in angels indicates people are looking for something real beyond this world. They know something is missing in their present lives; but unlike the coal miners, they just aren't sure what it is.

In this eerie, stomach-knotting silence, you have a window of opportunity to be a tool that God uses to change the world. It is the internal spiritual transformation of each believer that will turn the eyes of the world from angels to the God who created them. And it is God's use of your new spiritual DNA that will show them what is missing in their lives.

The study *Jesus by Heart* has been used to show you, step-by-step, how God, through the miracle of His Son, has given you a new identity — and thus freedom to become what you never thought you could be.

Your new spiritual DNA, the exact match of Jesus Christ's, floods your spirit. It gives you a new vision that will enable you to sing even when lions roar, because this world is not your home — it's just a stepping stone to eternity with God. By now you realize there is nothing you could have done to make this spiritual transformation happen. It is truly — and totally — a miracle of God. Every day, in some small way, He is transforming you into the likeness of Jesus. He cradles you in His loving arms and empowers you to love, trust, and obey Him with every step you make, every breath you take — just as Jesus did.

But with transformation comes responsibility. With His heart Jesus changed the world forever in His short time on earth. Now you are called to be an instrument for change in the world you live in during your time on earth. God will use you and your unique personality to evoke change — not because of *who* you are but because of *Whose* you are — His child, one who knows and loves Jesus by heart.

Just as Paul told Philemon that Onesimus was his very heart; just as God told the disciples that Jesus was His very heart; you are now the very heart of God. You are His emissary, His love letter to those who are searching for hope in a lost world.

"You show that you are a letter from Christ, the result of our ministry, written not with ink, but with the Spirit of the living God, not on tablets of stone but on tablets of human hearts" (2 Cor. 3:3).

Spiritual transformation is God's work of changing you into the likeness of Jesus by creating a new identity in Christ and by empowering a lifelong relationship of love, trust, and obedience to glorify God.

God has given you the answer to the questions the world is asking: He created you for relationship with Him. He will work through you to be the balm for those longing for peace. He will work through you to dry the silent tears of the lost. God will use you as His voice to tell others why they were born and what their lives are meant to accomplish. But you must speak now. You must answer the call: to live as Jesus lived, to love as Jesus loved, to obey as Jesus obeyed, to trust as Jesus trusted, and to glorify God as Jesus did. There is no greater mission. No higher calling. But the time is now. The window of opportunity is growing ever smaller. Your heart, transformed by God for a special purpose, must now become an intensely urgent heart.

Because the canary has stopped singing. And there is so much left to do.

This Is Your Life: *Write a Love Letter*

BY THE BOOK

Record the Bible verse that reflects your personal pledge to become just like Jesus.

_____

_____

_____

_____

_____

_____

Take a moment to share how God is transforming you to be like Jesus. Keep this as your personal letter of praise to God for the miraculous things He has done and continues to do in your life.

_____

_____

_____

_____

_____

_____

_____

_____

_____

_____

_____

_____

_____

_____

_____

_____

THE MAIN THING

What is the main thing you have learned from this study of *Jesus by Heart*?

_____

_____

_____

_____

_____

_____

_____

_____

_____

_____

_____

_____

_____

_____

_____

_____

_____

_____

A Moment with Jesus

"I am the vine, you are the branches. He who abides in Me, and I in him, bears much fruit; for without Me you can do nothing" (John 15:5, NKJV).

When Jesus spoke these words, He was revealing Himself as the nucleus of life — its very source. Jesus' power and love flowed from His perpetual fellowship with His Father. And it was evident in how Jesus lived every second of His life.

For you, *abiding in Christ* means an unbroken fellowship with Jesus — no separation. He is the source for your spiritual life and energy. The nourishment from Jesus cannot flow for a time, stop, and then flow again if you are to live the life He has planned for you. Instead, His nourishment to you must flow continuously, moment by moment. Because without His constant empowerment, you can do nothing.

When you abide moment by moment with Jesus, your life is so attached to Him that fruit has to come. And God is glorified by the fruit you bear. Jesus makes this clear in John 15:8 (NKJV): *"By this My Father is glorified, that you bear much fruit."* Jesus is saying that when you abide with Him daily, others will see Him flowing through you, and they'll hunger for what you have. They'll hunger for your healing touch just as those who walked this earth with Jesus hungered for His touch.

Can you really be in continuous contact with Jesus? Yes, you can. Following this "Moment with Jesus" is a special section on the life of Frank Laubach, a missionary and educator who decided to dedicate his life to being in contact with Jesus at all times — to live Jesus by heart. Doing so changed his life. And it will change yours. Take to heart the message of Jesus in John 15, just as you will see Frank Laubach took it to heart. Let this passage of Scripture become your guiding light for each day, for each moment of your life. For your life is nothing without Jesus.

Jesus Is the Source of Life

A Life Well Lived

Frank Laubach, born in the United States in 1884, was a missionary to the illiterate. His early years were dedicated to teaching others to read so they, too, could embrace the Word of God. But while Laubach was daily reaching out to others, he was dissatisfied with his own spiritual life and began, at age 45, recording in his diary his resolve to live in "continuous inner conversation with God and in perfect responsiveness to His will."[48]

Forty years later when Laubach took what was, for him, a very short step out of time into eternity, he was one of the most widely known and best-loved men of the 20th century. His accomplishments are endless, but the well-spring of this incredible man's life can be traced back to a lonely hill behind the shack where he lived in the Philippines on the island of Mindanao. It was there that Laubach wrote his experiences of daily seeking to constantly abide with Christ.

We have included some of Frank Laubach's journal entries here, and we prayerfully hope they will endure as long as there are Christians left upon this earth. As you read his own words, underline ways God enabled Frank Laubach to know Jesus by heart and to be in touch with Him at all times. This illustration is an example of one who learned to follow Jesus by heart. It answers the question—can I know, love, and live Jesus by heart?

January 20, 1930

"Although I have been a minister and a missionary for fifteen years, I have not lived the entire day of every day, minute by minute to follow the will of God. Two years ago a profound dissatisfaction led me to begin trying to line up my actions with the will of God about every 15 minutes or every half hour. Other people to whom I confessed this intention said it was impossible. I judge from what I have heard that few people are really trying even that. But this year I have started out to live all my waking moments in conscious listening to the inner voice, asking without ceasing, "What, Father, do you desire said? What, Father, do you desire this minute?" It is clear that this is exactly what Jesus was doing all day every day."

January 29, 1930

"I feel simply carried along each hour, doing my part in a plan which is far beyond myself. This sense of cooperation with God in little things is what so astonishes me, for I never felt it this way before. I need something, and turn around to find it waiting for me. I must work, to be sure, but there is God working along with me. God takes care of all the rest. My part is to live this hour in continuous inner conversation with God and in perfect responsiveness to his will, to make this hour gloriously rich. This seems to be all I need to think about."

March 1, 1930

"The sense of being led by an unseen hand which takes mine while another hand reaches ahead and prepares the way, grows upon me daily. I do not need to strain at all to find opportunity. It piles in upon as the waves roll over the beach, and yet there is time to do something about opportunity. Perhaps a man who has been an ordained minister since 1914 ought to be ashamed to confess that he never before felt the joy of complete hourly, minute by minute —now what shall I call it? — more than surrender. I had that before. More than listening to God. I tried that before. I cannot find the word that will mean to you or to me what I am now experiencing. It is a *will* act. I compel my mind to open straight out toward God. I wait and listen with determined sensitiveness. I fix my attention there, and sometimes it requires a long time early in the morning. I determine not to get out of bed until that mind set upon the Lord is settled. After a while, perhaps, it will become a habit, and the sense of effort will grow less."

March 23, 1930

"One question now to be put to test is this: Can we have that contact with God all the time? All the time awake, fall asleep in His arms, and awaken in His presence? Can we attain that? Can we do His will all the time? Can we think His thoughts all the time?"

April 18, 1930

"I have tasted a thrill in fellowship with God, which has made anything discordant with God disgusting. This afternoon the possession of God has caught me up with such sheer joy that I thought I never had known anything like it. God was so close and so amazingly lovely that I felt like melting all over with a strange blissful contentment. Having had this experience, which comes to me now several times a week, the thrill of filth repels me, for I know its power to drag me from God. And after an hour of close friendship with God my soul feels clean, as new fallen snow."

May 14, 1930

"Oh, this thing of keeping in constant touch with God, of making Him the object of my thought and the companion of my conversations, is the most amazing thing I ever ran across. It is working. I cannot do it even half of a day — not yet, but I believe I shall be doing it some day for the entire day. It is a matter of acquiring a new habit of thought. Now I like the Lord's presence so much that when for a half hour or so He slips out of mind — as He does many times a day — I feel as though I had deserted Him, and as though I had lost something very precious in my life."

June 1, 1930

"Last Monday was the most completely successful day of my life to date, so far as giving my day in complete and continuous surrender to God is concerned — though I hope for far better days — and I remember how as I looked at people with a love God gave, they looked back and acted as though they wanted to go with me. I felt then that for a day I saw a little of that marvelous pull that Jesus had as He walked along the road day after day 'God-intoxicated' and radiant with the endless communion of His soul with God."[49]

A Word from the Authors

Frank Laubach found a great truth in his journey. He learned that he had an unlimited capacity to grow spiritually in his relationship with God. You have that same unlimited capacity. There is no boundary to what you can become as you yield your life to constantly abiding in Jesus. As you conclude your study of *Jesus by Heart*, may you seek, as Frank Laubach did, to walk along the road of your life, day-after-day, moment-by-moment, "God intoxicated" and radiant with the endless communion of your soul with God. God bless you as you follow this path to know, love, and live Jesus by Heart.

Roy T Edgemon   *Barry Sneed*

A Note from the Publisher:

As fellow believers, we would love to hear how God is working in your life to transform you into the likeness of Jesus. If you would like to share your personal story of transformation with us, please send it, along with your name, address, and phone number to:

Jesus by Heart
127 Ninth Avenue North
Nashville, TN 37234-0150

You can also fax us at 615-251-3851
or email us at bsneed@lifeway.com

If you give permission for your story to be published in a future Lifeway publication as a testimony of God at work in the life of a believer, please sign here and date your signature. We will notify you if it is being published.

Signature _____

Date _____

Name Printed _____

Street Address _____

City, State, Zip Code _____

Phone Number _____

Email Address _____

Next Steps for Spiritual Transformation

The next step for spiritual transformation is to stay in God's Word. Another suggestion would be to go through *Jesus by Heart* again. Pray about leading a small-group through *Jesus by Heart*.

The following resources will serve as excellent tools to assist you in your continued study of God's Word. Each of these resources may be studied individually or in a small-group.

Transformational Discipleship: Your Church Helping People Be Like Jesus by Barry Sneed and Henry Webb – This resource will help church leaders develop or strengthen the discipleship ministry of their church. It will assist churches, regardless of size or situation, to create an environment and build a foundation for spiritual transformation. The environment for transformation maintains a focus on our relationship with Jesus. God is at work changing a believer into the likeness of Jesus by creating a new identity in Christ and by empowering a lifelong relationship of love, trust, and obedience to glorify God. (Available August 1999)

My Identity in Christ by Gene Wilkes — This resource will help new and mature Christians know who they are in Christ. It can help powerfully change how new believers see themselves, the church, and God's purposes in their lives. It is the first step in the journey to be transformed into the likeness of Christ. (Available December 1999)

Experiencing God: Knowing and Doing the Will of God by Henry Blackaby – This resource helps Christians experience God doing through them what only God can do.

The Mind of Christ by T. W. Hunt – This course provides help for learning to think the thoughts of Christ. It is based on Philippians 2:5-11: *"Let this mind be in you, which was also in Christ Jesus."*

Life in the Spirit by Robertson McQuilkin – This biblical study of the Holy Spirit's power and activities helps Christians experience a deep and loving relationship with God, effectiveness in personal living, and ministry that makes a difference in our world.

Living Beyond Yourself by Beth Moore – Through this in-depth study of the fruit of the Spirit, Beth challenges you to pursue the only route to develop the fruit by maintaining an intimate relationship with the Spirit of God. As you walk with God, He develops in you the fruit of the Spirit.

To Live Is Christ by Beth Moore – This in-depth study of the life of Paul will challenge believers to follow Paul's example of following the example of Jesus.

The Man God Uses: Moved from the Ordinary to the Extraordinary by Henry and Tom Blackaby – This seven-chapter study of Scripture clearly shows how men who have encountered God need to understand what He is doing in their lives: personal, family, work, church, and community.

MasterLife: A Biblical Process for Growing Disciples by Avery T. Willis, Jr. – This classic study is in a format of four six-week workbooks. As believers learn to practice six biblical disciplines, Jesus transforms their behavior; leads them to develop kingdom values; and involves them in His mission in the home, the church, and the world.

Jesus on Leadership: Becoming a Servant Leader by Gene Wilkes – This six-lesson study encourages believers to follow Jesus' example and teachings on servant leadership. Participants discover how God prepares them for ministry through their spiritual gifts, life experiences, relational style, vocational skills, and enthusiasm. This is a terrific tool to equip leaders and develop team ministries.

Share Jesus Without Fear by William Fay and Ralph Hodge – This evangelistic resource is an approach for sharing Jesus depending upon the power of the Holy Spirit and the Bible with no Scripture memory required. It helps participants overcome the fears of failure and rejection by obeying Jesus.

Each of these resources is available by calling 1-800-458-2772; writing the Customer Service Center, 127 Ninth Avenue North, Nashville, TN 37234-0113; visiting the nearest LifeWay Christian Store; faxing 1-615-251-5933; emailing customerservice@lifeway.com; or visiting our Internet website – www.lifeway.com.

Footnotes

1. As told by Ralph Hodge. Gallatin, Tennessee. Used by permission.

2. As told by Ralph Hodge. Gallatin, Tennessee. Used by permission.

3. Max Lucado, *Just Like Jesus* (Nashville: Word Publishing, a Thomas Nelson Company, 1998), 3.

4. "Mary, Did You Know?" Words by Buddy Greene. Music by Mark Lowry. Copyright © 1991 Rufus Music and Word Music. All rights reserved. Used By Permission.

5. From *The Way of Holiness* by Stephen Olford, copyright © 1998. Used by permission of Good News Publishers/Crossway Books, Wheaten, Illinois 60187.

6. As told by Ralph Hodge. Gallatin, Tennessee. Used by permission.

7. As quoted in 1965 seminar by Roy Williams, Professor of New Testament, Cumberland College, Williamsburg, KY, to Ralph Hodge.

8. Mary E. Byrne and Eleanor H. Hull, words. David Evans, music. "Be Thou My Vision," Copyright © 1927, *Revised Church Hymnary*, Oxford University Press. Reprinted from *The Baptist Hymnal*, 1991, 60.

9. Adapted from *The Life God Blesses, Weathering the Storms of Life That Threaten the Soul* by Gordon McDonald (Nashville: Thomas Nelson Publishers, 1994), 1-5.

10. John Trent, Ph.d., "The Whisper Test" *Men of Action,* Winter 1993, 5. Used by permission.

11. From *The Message.* © 1993, 1994, 1995 by Eugene Peterson. Used by permission of NavPress, Colorado Springs, CO. All rights reserved. For copies call (800) 366-7788.

12. Dallas Willard, "Life in God" Voice of the Vineyard, Winter 1998, 11-14.

13. From *How Can I Help?* by Ram Dass and Paul Gorman. Copyright © 1985 by Ram Dass and Paul Gorman. Reprinted by permission of Alfred A. Knopf, Inc.

14. From *A Long Obedience in the Same Direction* by Eugene Peterson. © 1980 InterVarsity Christian Fellowship/USA. Used by permission of InterVarsity Press, P. O. Box 1400, Downers Grove, IL 60515.

15. "Shine, Jesus, Shine," copyright © 1989 Make Way Music Ltd.,(adm. in N, S, C America by Integrity's Hosanna! Music)/ ASCAP. All rights reserved. International copyright secured. Used by permission c/o Integrity Music, 1000 Cody Road, Mobile, AL 36695.

16. As told by Ralph Hodge. Gallatin, Tennessee. Used by permission.

17. *My Life* © 1993 Columbia Pictures Industries, Inc. All Rights Reserved. © 1994 Layout and Design Columbia TriStar Home Video. All Rights Reserved.

18. Henry Ward Beecher, *A Dictionary of Thoughts,* by Tryon Edwards, D.D. (Detriot: F. B. Dickerson Co., 1915), 363.

19. George Mueller, *Soul Nourishment First* (Los Angeles: Bible House of Los Angeles, 1900).

20. "Where the Silence Breaks," written by Phil Naish, Lowell Alexander, Dave Clark, and Tony Wood. © 1998 Randy Cox Music, Inc. /BMI/Word Music/Meadowgreen Music (Adm. by EMI Christian Music Publishing/ASCAP/International copyright secured. All Rights Reserved. Used by permission.

21. Albert C. Outler, ed., *The Works of John Wesley, Vol. 1* (Nashville: Abingdon Press, United Methodist Publishing House, 1984), 105. Used by permission.

22. Ivy Harrington, *Home Again,* © Copyright 1999.

23. As told to Barry Sneed and Sam House, LifeWay Christian Resources, Nashville, Tennessee. Used by permission.

24. From *The Life You've Always Wanted* by John Ortberg. Copyright © 1997 by John Ortberg. Used by permission of Zondervan Publishing House.
25. Ibid.
26. Ivey Harrington, *Home Again,* © Copyright 1999.
27. Origin Unknown.
28. Adapted from *Sensei; The Life Story of Irene Webster-Smith* by Russell T. Hitt (London: Hodder and Stoughton, 1966).
29. Ernest J. Gaines, *The Autobiography of Miss Jane Pittman,* (New York: Bantam Books, a division of Doubleday, Dell Publishing Group, a division of Random House, Inc., 1971), 213.
30. "Make Us One" by Carol Cymbala. Copyright © 1991 Carol Joy Music/ASCAP (Admin. by ICG)/Word Music/ASCAP. All Rights Reserved. Used By Permission.
31. Adapted from the movie *Smoke,* Miramax Films a division of HOF/EuroSpace Productions.
32. Edward Young, "Welcome to Ali's Domain"(http://home.bip.net/azadi/quotes.htm).
33. Adapted from speech given by Robertson McQuilkin, during December Meeting 1996, LifeWay Christian Resources. Used by permission.
34. Adapted from *God's Little Devotional Book,* (Tulsa, OK: Honor Books, Inc., 1995), 83. Used by permission.
35. Ibid., 109.
36. Sy Safransky, *Four in the Morning,* (New York: Bantam Doubleday Dell, 1993).
37. Paul S. Rees, *The Adequate Man* (London: Marshall Pickering, division of Harper Collins,1958), 107.
38. J. H. Jowett, *The High Calling,* (New York: Revell,1909), 202.
39. Earl F. Palmer, *The Communicator's Commentary, 1,2,3 John; Revelation* (Waco, TX: Word Books Publisher, 1982),139.
40. Adapted from *God's Little Devotional Book* (Tulsa, OK: Honor Books, Inc., 1995), 197. Used by permission.
41. From *They Rose Above It* by Bob Considine. Copyright © 1977 by Millie Considine as Executive of the Estate of Bob Considine. Used by permission of Doubleday, a division of Random House, Inc.
42. As told by Ralph Hodge, Gallatin, Tennessee. Used by permission.
43. As told by Roy Edgemon, Director of Discipleship and Family Group, LifeWay Christian Resources, Nashville, Tennessee. Used by permission.
44. As told to Clint Kelly by Talmage Wilson. Used by permission.
45. Penny Lea, "Sing a LIttle Louder," *Journal of The American Society for Church Growth,* Gary L. McIntosh, ed. (La Mirada, CA: 1997), Appendix II.
46. Origin Unknown.
47. As told by Ralph Hodge, Gallatin, Tennessee. Used by permission.
48. Brother Lawrence and Frank Laubach, *Practicing His Presence,* 1973, xiii-xiv. New Readers Press, U.S. Publishing Division of Laubach Literacy. Used by permission.
49. Ibid., 2, 5-6, 10, 13, 15, 19.

Conducting a Group Study
of Jesus by Heart

The Leader's Guide on the following pages includes:
- Group Leader Ideas
- Weekly Group Session Plans (pp. 129-142)

Read every section before you plan for your group's meetings.

Group Leader Ideas

Who?   A group study of *Jesus By Heart* is appropriate for any discipleship, prayer, or cell group, or one-to-one discipling. The study will benefit adult believers of all ages.

When?   Meet at a time (and place) appropriate for your group. Sessions can be conducted within 50-60 minutes. Group plans in this section serve as a framework; your goal should be to meet the learning needs of those in your group.

How?   Use the weekly group session plans. Before each session, as group leader you should:
- Pray for each group member.
- Complete and prepare material for that week.
- Encourage each group member.
- Contact those who missed the previous session.

God bless you as you allow Him to direct you.

Session One
Introduction

The first group session is a time of distributing the book, summarizing the purpose of the material, and understanding the format for the group session each week. The following list will help you.

1. Begin on time to demonstrate your commitment to the group and the message. As the group arrives give each person a copy of the book.

2. Open with a prayer for God's leadership. Then read the excerpt from Paul's letter to the Romans (Rom. 12:1-2) found on page 7.

3. Ask the group for examples of how someone could offer themselves as living sacrifices, holy and pleasing to God. Accept all responses as contributions to the discussion. Share the example from the first paragraph on page 9.

4. Ask the group to turn to page 7 and follow silently as you read again the second half of the Romans passage to them.

5. Say, "God knows us by knowing our heart, and we know God by knowing His heart. To know Jesus is to know the heart of God. The heart of God is that believers be transformed into the likeness of Jesus. The goal of this study, and of our group, is to grasp the need for each person to have an intimate, personal relationship with Jesus that changes believers' hearts and transforms them into new persons."

6. Invite each member of the group to make a commitment to read each daily study and complete the exercises. Point out that Week 1 is an extremely practical, in-depth look at what it means to know God through Jesus Christ.

7. Tell the group that one of the greatest benefits of going through this study together is getting to know better their brothers and sisters in Christ. Ask each one to briefly tell who he or she is, one reason why he or she came to the introductory session, and one expectation he or she has of the study.

8. Ask participants to read in unison the definition of spiritual transformation in bold print on page 10. Then invite the group to talk about the implications of that definition for their lives. (Write the definition on a poster that you can place on the wall each week.)

9. Close the session with prayer. Linger briefly to invite opportunity for getting better acquainted with group members or to answer any questions.

Session Two
Week 1: The Heart of Your Faith

1. Begin on time. Warmly greet individuals as they arrive. Provide name tags during the first group session unless the group members know each other well. Have the name tags easily accessible to arriving members so that latecomers can get theirs and be seated with the least inconvenience for them or the group.

2. Ask the group to be seated for a demonstration. Ask the group to close their eyes. Then say, "Hypothetically, if I asked you, keeping your eyes closed, to search this room for a mark I had made on the floor, you would have trouble finding it. You could theorize and try your hardest, but without ending your blindness, you would never find my mark. At times, you may have felt as if you were blindly groping your way to God. But, just as sight removes the obstacle that kept you from finding my mark, only Jesus can remove the obstacle of sin that keeps you from knowing God. Looking in any other direction, stumbling in the dark, only limits you in finding what it means to know God." Remind them of the quote in the margin on page 11, "Every barrier has been removed between you and knowing God."

3. With their eyes still closed, ask the group to ask themselves, "Have I come to the point in my life where I've realized that Jesus is the only way to remove the sin barrier between God and me?" Pause for a full minute, then ask the group to turn to one or two others, making sure no one is left alone, and describe what it feels like to be forgiven. Remind them of the prayer printed on page 13. They may wish to review it as they recall the forgiveness they received when they called upon Christ for forgiveness. Allow two or three minutes. Give a one-minute warning before ending the discussion.

4. Summarize for the group saying, "The core of your faith is that God saved you by sending His Son to die for your sins, so that you can have a relationship with God. A relationship with God brings a miraculous transformation that changes your character, your nature, and your perspective. His love changes you when you allow Him to remove the barrier of sin and live through you. The Bible says knowing Jesus means that we know God (Col. 1:15-23)." Read aloud The Main Thing on page 22, "God has wiped away your past and given you the freedom and the power to be everything He wants you to be." Ask the group what implications this statement has for their lives.

5. Say to the group, "Paul knew *about* God when he was persecuting Christians. Then

Paul met Jesus and came to *know* God. What is different in your life because you know God instead of only knowing about God? Turn to your partner(s) and discuss your response to this question."

6. Remind the group that it is vital to our relationship with God to ask Him to remove anything that would keep Him from changing us from the inside out. Ask, "What are some things that might scare someone from knowing God more intimately?" Allow the group to respond. Silence is not necessarily a sign to move on. If more than a minute passes, be prepared to start the discussion with one brief example of a fear someone might have about getting closer to anyone, then ask how that could apply to knowing God more intimately.

7. Read The Main Thing on page 28, "Christians hold in their hearts a vision of certainty and hope that those without Jesus can never know." Ask the group to remember when and how they came to know Jesus. Being able to tell someone, in one or two minutes, about the start of their new life in Christ is how believers can obey Jesus by being His witnesses. Direct the small discussion groups to form again and share their experiences in one or two minutes.

8. Point out the "And in Closing..." section that appears at the end of this week's chapter. Ask the group to discuss their responses to the most important thing God has taught them through this week's study and what action God wants them to take. Add the group's comments about what God has taught them to a list of truths on a tear sheet or chalkboard that can be updated with the group's input each week. Refer to the definition of spiritual transformation on the poster.

9. Dismiss by praying a prayer of thanksgiving for each one in the group.

Session Three
Week 2: Your Transformed Heart

1. Begin on time. To emphasize the contrast between outward activities while neglecting inner transformation, consider having aerobics routine music playing as the group arrives.

2. Remark that rather than just being big, luxurious boats, some yachts are sleek, beautiful, examples of the shipbuilder's craft. Briefly recount the tragic story of Michael Plant, whose state-of-the-art yacht capsized when it lost its keel weight and could no longer balance in the water. As beautiful as the craft still was, even floating upside-down, it couldn't do what it was made for or even carry its captain. Ask the group to reflect on how their spiritual keels can keep their lives in balance.

3. Point out to the group how only God can take our forgiven, forever-changed hearts and transform our entire beings into Christlikeness. Ask the group to listen as you read the quote on page 33, "There is a danger of giving attention to the outward activities of spiritual life while neglecting the inner transformation of the heart that comes with an intimate relationship with Jesus." Discuss what the group understands to be the consequences of neglecting the inner transformation that comes with an intimate relationship with Jesus.

4. Ask the group how some of them have decided to discontinue some of the activity in their schedules to be available to the Spirit's activity in their lives.

5. Ask them to list ways that they could be encouraged or encourage group members in making the sacrifices necessary to not compete with what God wants to do in their lives.

6. Ask the group, by surrendering their lives to God, how they have experienced God changing the way they experience the list on pages 37 and 38.

7. Say to the group, "Jesus said, 'If you really knew me, you would know my Father as well.' What is Jesus doing in your life that would allow people to know Him, or at least, more about Him?"

8. On page 39, love is called the root command of the Bible. Remind the group that when the Bible commands that we love, it isn't talking about the "easy" love that we can make available to sweet children, good friends, and dear spouses. The command

is to love those who may even despise us. This is God's unconditional, *agape* love.

9. Discuss Jesus' response to those who tried and crucified Him and why He would die to save them, too. What are the implications for followers of Jesus today? Jesus' response illustrated the relationship of love, trust, and obedience He had with the Father.

10. Say to the group, "Truly loving Jesus means committing yourself to trust Him. Loving the people we find hard to love requires trusting Jesus' love for them. Pair up and discuss your responses about trust in the exercise on page 43."

11. On page 46, 2 Corinthians 3:18 is applied in this way, "God's full intention is to call to Himself a people born of the Spirit, people who live life empowered by love, trust, and obedience, and who's only joy is in glorifying God." Ask, "What are some ways this group believes God's glory is being reflected from us?" Discuss.

12. Point out the "And in Closing..." section on page 48. Ask the group to discuss their responses to the most important thing God has taught them through this week's study and what action God wants them to take. Add the group's comments about what God has taught them to the list of truths the group began after studying Week 1. Dismiss with prayer.

Session Four
Week 3: Strengthening Your Heart

1. Greet each group member with a small ball of clay or other children's modeling material. Ask them to turn their lumps of clay into something and place their creations on some newspaper you have laid out.

2. Begin on time. Quote, from page 49, "Much of the trouble in your life may be simply part of living in an imperfect world. The effect, however—to transform you into the likeness of Jesus—is a work of the Holy Spirit." Ask the group, "What in life prepared you to shape your clay (things you have seen, touched, experienced before)? What did you use to shape your clay?" Remind the group that God uses various tools to bring about spiritual transformation in our lives.

3. Point out that God's Word is a transformational power source. Ask the group to turn to the Scripture passages on page 50 and 51. As they read them and think about each one, ask them to consider the transforming power in each verse and how it impacts their lives. After a few moments, interrupt the silence by reading the lyrics to *When the Silence Breaks,* found on page 51. Discuss with the group what it means to be "weak enough to listen and strong enough to wait."

4. Pair up participants and ask them to share their responses from "Wisdom of the Ages" on page 54. Ask the pairs to conclude by praying together over any resistance to godly wisdom that they may have found.

5. Ask the group to discuss their individual responses to the story of Joe Nu'u, the angry teenager who met Christ through someone who showed him the love of Christ (pp. 55-56). On page 57, participants identified two people in the church that God used to " sharpen your faith and prepare you for ministry." Invite the group to share their responses.

6. Remind the group of the paragraph on page 59 that states, "Spiritual exercises are the resources God uses to strengthen your love for Him and all people." Ask what some of their responses were to the exercise on page 60 that asks about what spiritual exercises God is currently using to shape each of them. After allowing for discussion, summarize by saying that whatever we are involved in to strengthen us spiritually, holiness is an activity of God (Heb. 2:11).

7. Continue the discussion by asking the group to respond to The Main Thing stated

on page 61, "Spiritual exercises are not the barometer of spirituality; they are the means by which you place your life as an offering before God so that He can create holiness in you." After you read the statement aloud to the group, ask for their comments.

8. Ask what new opportunities for growth they have today that they did not have (or recognize) two years ago. Discuss. Ask which of the "Exercising Outside of the Box" disciplines (p. 61) do they believe God may be leading them toward? Encourage the group to think of other disciplines.

9. Review "A Moment with Jesus" on page 65. Ask the group to comment on the five factors listed for going deeper with God.

10. Point out the "And in Closing..." section that appears at the end of this week's chapter. Ask the group to discuss their responses to the most important thing God has taught them through this week's study and what action God wants them to take. Add the group's comments about what God has taught them to the list of truths the group has listed after studying Week 1 and Week 2. Dismiss with prayer.

Session Five
Week 4: Your Visible Heart

1. Greet each member of the group with a compliment about something in their character that reflects Christ's presence. For example, "Joe, your faith in God always lifts me up. Kim, I believe people can tell that you have the peace of God in your heart."

2. Begin on time. Hold up a good-looking fresh flower, leafy plant, ripe vegetable, or piece of fruit. Say, "I can enjoy this example of God's creation. But who would think from looking at it that garbage could help it be this beautiful? Dead weeds and grass, vegetable peelings, egg shells—even manure, can make soil so rich, it can't help but grow the best examples of what the Creator has created for us. A plant can't trust that when someone puts garbage around it, the garbage will help it grow. In our lives, trust in God is what makes the difference when we face what looks like garbage to us. When we trust God, others observe and receive hope from the love for God that they see in us."

3. Ask the group to turn to "This Is Your Life: Beyond the Jagged Edge," on page 71. Ask members to pair up and discuss their descriptions of something they have always dreamed of doing.

4. Remind the group that decisions we make affect our relationship with Jesus. Ask the group to reflect on, and then discuss, decisions they have made during the past week that allowed God to shine through their lives.

5. According to John 17:11, Jesus desires unity in the body. Criticism and bickering are not helpful to a congregation trying to be one in God's Spirit. Read aloud John 17:11 to the group, "I will remain in the world no longer, but they are still in the world, and I am coming to you. Holy Father, protect them by the power of your name—the name you gave me—so that they will be one as we are one."

6. Ask them for their thoughts on how a congregation finds the joint focus on Jesus' goal of unity in the church? Ask the group to list ways God is glorified through a congregation when the love of Jesus overcomes the human traits of envy, jealousy, frustration, and selfishness.

7. Say, "God has made us each unique. When we come together as the body of Christ, though we share the same Spirit with the rest of the body, there will be diversity that glorifies God. Consider our small group. What are some unique aspects of this part of

the body of Christ? How might God use this unique combination to serve His purposes?" Discuss.

8. Under "This Is Your Life: Express Yourself" (p. 82). There are two questions about what keeps us from being what God has created us to be. Ask the group to form pairs or triads to discuss their thoughts on these questions.

9. Point out the "And in Closing..." section on page 84. Ask the group to discuss their responses to the most important thing God has taught them through this week's study and what action God wants them to take. Add the group's comments about what God has taught them to the list of truths from previous sessions.

10. At the end of Week 4 in this book, "A Moment with Jesus" ends with the thought, "My heart has plenty of room for you." Make the surrender of self-centeredness the subject of a time of sentence prayers to end the session.

Session Six
Week 5: Enemies of Your Heart

1. Before the session, enlist someone in the group who would be willing to read aloud the illustration that begins Day Four, on page 96 about Martha, Mary, and Jesus.

2. As group members arrive, give each of them a roll of round, flavored candies. Tell them the candy is to remind them that Jesus is their life-saver. He is always with us.

3. Begin on time. Remind the group of Robertson McQuilkin's childhood story on page 85. Open by giving God the credit for preserving peace in your life this week or for delivering you from life's spiritual bullies. Invite others to share similar accounts.

4. Conclude by quoting from page 85, "Your Heavenly Father is always with you. His Holy Spirit lifts you up when you're down, guides you when you're lost, cautions you when you're tempted, restores you when you fall, laughs with you when things go right, and weeps with you when things go wrong."

5. Tell the group, "The opposite of self-centeredness is God-centeredness." Encourage someone in the group to provide an example of the difference. Ask the group if they have had a chance to think about the difference between being selfish and being a servant. Invite them to pair-up and give each other one example of a servant-moment and a selfish-moment that they have had recently. Ask them to discuss with their partner how things might have gone differently if they always approached life with a servant's heart.

6. Read aloud 1 John 5:4, *"For everyone born of God overcomes the world. This is the victory that has overcome the world, even our faith."* Tell the group that Satan would like us to live under the deception that when circumstances seem bad, God is not with us. God's Word says otherwise. Refer to the questions on page 91. Discuss the group's responses to those times when God's grace saw them through. Read the 1 John passage aloud again to summarize the discussion.

7. Point out that Scripture is an invaluable message from God to us. It contains His message and our instructions. To reinforce our need for God's Word, invite the group to turn to "This Is Your Life" on page 92. Ask them to share any thoughts that the exercise caused them to reflect upon. Discuss.

8. During the session, ask the group to listen with eyes closed as the enlisted person reads the illustration. Ask the group to imagine themselves as Martha. Point out that distractions can turn our hearts from grace and mercy to legalistic self-righteousness.

9. Remind the group that although Jesus has already, definitely, won the victory over all the attacks of Satan against believers, threats can still disturb us. Ask the group to share the things that seem like the worst threats believers have to face.

10. Remind the group that God has made His strength available through Jesus Christ. Ask the group to turn to the Ephesians 6:10-18 passage, found in the margins on pages 98-99. Ask them to read those verses to themselves, underlining all of the expressions of action, such as "be strong" and "put on," that they find there. Go through the passage with the group, sharing the words they underlined. Ask the group to discuss how meditating on this passage each morning could help them get ready to live the day serving Christ.

11. Point out the "And in Closing..." section on page 101. Ask the group to discuss their responses to the most important thing God has taught them through this week's study and what action God wants them to take. Add the group's comments about what God has taught them to the list of truths from previous sessions.

12. Have the group join hands as you offer a prayer for their peace and confidence as they trust the promises of Jesus. Dismiss.

Session Seven
Week 6: Your Urgent Heart

1. Before the session, have blank tear sheets or some way of writing things to be seen by the whole group.

2. As the group arrives, greet each one by pressing a cotton ball into each one's hand.

3. Begin on time. Holding a cotton ball in the open palm of your hand, say, "This barely weighs anything. It could fall on you and you might not even notice. Some of these little balls are still made from the seed pod fibers of cotton plants. Some are synthetic. Either way, these little puffs don't give many hints that they have come from fields of living plants or barrels of oil or chemicals.

"Each of us have something in common with these gobs of fiber. Like the baby, Ngo Thi Lam (pp. 103-104), what others see, or how we seem, may give few clues about where we have been and the pain we have experienced. Those who become silent weepers are the result of pain and loneliness so great that hope of anyone caring is gone. Only God's love can rescue silent weepers. You and I must care because our new hearts hold Jesus' response to a world in pain. We cannot rescue them, but we can bring them to the One who rescued us. We can love them because God loves us."

4. Point out to the group that in crises, people would be shocked if rescue workers and paramedics stopped to flip through a magazine or take a nap before helping the victims. The workers might explain that they needed to read an article about crises, or that they knew they could be stronger if they got some extra rest. However, when the need is urgent, these reasons become excuses.

Ask the group to come up with excuses that people offer for not being totally committed to sharing the love of Jesus. Record their responses so that the whole group can see them, or at least have them read back to the group. Remind the group that excuses can be like clear plastic wrap that allows people to see what is sealed inside, but never come in contact with what is sealed inside. Ask someone to voice a prayer for the group, asking God's forgiveness for letting thin excuses keep us from sharing the love and the urgency of Christ with the world.

5. Say, "A forgiven heart leads to a transformed life. A life that is transformed, and being transformed, by Jesus bears witness to His presence by obeying Him." Ask the group to tell you or read together the words of The Great Commission (Matt. 28:19-20, p. 106). Separate the commands to go, make disciples, baptize, and teach. Lead the group in a prayer meditation as you guide them to pray for someone they should

take Jesus to, someone they could help grow in Christ, someone they could unwrap their witness for and feed them the truth of God's love, and to thank God for those who have sacrificed in order to do these things for them.

6. Ask the group to talk about impossible times or tasks they have faced. Ask them about God's power to do what is impossible for us to do. Share the testimony of the Wortens (p. 108), or call for testimonies of God's power to overcome.

Point out the truth of Psalm 46:1, *"God is our refuge and strength, an ever-present help in trouble"* (p. 109). Say the verse for them, then lead the group to repeat it together. End with an "Amen!"

7. Remind the group that when they gave their lives to Christ, "something" inside of them could not resist surrendering to God's love and truth. That something was God, drawing them to Him. Say, "If we believe that we are responsible for convincing people to come to Jesus, we are stuck in a worldly way of looking at salvation. God is already at work, going before us (John 6:44). He invites us to celebrate our freedom by seeing Him set others free." Read John 8:32 aloud to the group, *"Then you will know the truth and the truth will set you free."*

8. Review the "And in Closing..." list of responses they have been making throughout the study (pp. 31, 48, 66, 84, and 101). Tell them that the truths they have realized, and what God wants them to do, are part of the transformation God is working in their lives. Ask the group to discuss any differences they notice in their lives or thinking over the past few weeks.

Remind them that it is the internal spiritual transformation of believers that will allow them to see the world through the lens of Scripture. Changed lives will turn the eyes of the world to God and show them what is missing in their lives.

9. Remind the group of the letter each wrote during the week (p. 118). Let each person reflect on that letter. Remind them of Frank Laubach's hunger to be in a continuous inner conversation with God, his responsiveness to God's will, and his passion to be obedient to God.

10. To close, lead the group in a time of guided prayer. Say, "You are God's love letter to the world. Ask God to show you what your life is saying to others right now." Pause, then continue. "Who are you aware of that you could bring hope to by introducing them to Jesus?" Pause again, then continue. "Recommit your heart to God and whatever special purpose He has for your life." Pause, and conclude by reading the last paragraph on page 122 ("A Word from the Authors").

CHRISTIAN GROWTH STUDY PLAN

Preparing Christians to Serve

In the Christian Growth Study Plan *Jesus by Heart: God Can Transform You to Be Like Jesus* is a resource for course credit in one of the Leadership and Skill development diploma plans. It is also a resource in the Christian Growth category subject area Personal Life. To receive credit in a group study that is 2.5 hours or more, attend the sessions and read the book. To receive credit for individual study, read the book; complete the learning activities; and show your work to your pastor, a staff member, or a church leader.

This page may be duplicated. Send the completed page to:

Christian Growth Study Plan
127 Ninth Avenue North
Nashville, TN 37234-0117
Fax (615) 251-5067

For information about the Christian Growth Study Plan, refer to the current *Christian Growth Study Plan Catalog.* Your church office may have a copy. If not, request a free copy from the Christian Growth Study Plan office, (615) 251-2525.

Jesus by Heart: God Can Transform You to Be Like Jesus
COURSE NUMBER: CG-0497

PARTICIPANT INFORMATION

Social Security Number (USA ONLY) | Personal CGSP Number* | Date of Birth (MONTH, DAY, YEAR)

Name (First, Middle, Last)
☐ Mr. ☐ Miss
☐ Mrs. ☐

Home Phone

Address (Street, Route, or P.O. Box) | City, State, or Province | Zip/Postal Code

CHURCH INFORMATION

Church Name

Address (Street, Route, or P.O. Box) | City, State, or Province | Zip/Postal Code

CHANGE REQUEST ONLY

☐ Former Name

☐ Former Address | City, State, or Province | Zip/Postal Code

☐ Former Church | City, State, or Province | Zip/Postal Code

Signature of Pastor, Conference Leader, or Other Church Leader | Date

*New participants are requested but not required to give SS# and date of birth. Existing participants, please give CGSP# when using SS# for the first time.
 Thereafter, only one ID# is required. **Mail to:** Christian Growth Study Plan, 127 Ninth Ave., North, Nashville, TN 37234-0117. Fax: (615)251-5067